Hafa Gachong
Letters to the Commonwealth

Written by

Ramon Garrido Villagomez

Edited by

Angelo O'Connor Villagomez

ISBN: 978-1719052955
ISBN-13: 1719052956

INTRO ABOUT MY DAD

My dad died way too young. For everything that he accomplished in his 50 years, that's the story of his life. I was only 21 when he had the heart attack. He never fully recovered, never spoke again, and eventually passed five years later. I wish he was the one sharing these letters with you. In fact, I wish he was still writing them. The next best thing is for me to share them with you.

Dad was a prolific writer. Later in life, when he was a Commonwealth of Northern Mariana Islands Supreme Court Justice and Chair of the Board of Regents of the Northern Mariana Islands College, his words carried heft. They were deliberate. The whole community read them and heeded his words. Early in his career? Not so much.

He wrote his first letter to the editor in September, 1972, about 2 weeks shy of his 23rd birthday. He was already a young father at the time, supporting a small family. He was about to head to law school in Washington, DC.

His early letters intrigue me. It is not common in our culture for people in their twenties to put their opinions out into the public realm so freely. Nobody cares what you have to say until you are in your forties. There are a few young folk who follow in his footsteps today, myself included, but back then this was unheard of. Despite his age, his writings fell on fertile ears. Family members still talk to me today about the letters they remember reading in the 1970s. As of this writing, that was forty years ago. It is not a stretch to suggest that his letters have had an impact on life in the Commonwealth today, just as they did back then. Amazingly enough, many of the issues he ponders still persist in the community.

In this book I've compiled most of his letters from the 1970s, starting with his first letter in 1972 as a young man about to head off to law school, to letters in 1979 when he is a practicing attorney, raising his second family (that's where I come into the story).

I present his letters in somewhat of a jumble, but there is an order to my madness. His early letters are written from the point of view of a law student, so I offer those first. To be honest, they aren't very good. You can tell that his writing improves as you read each successive letter. Many of his writings are political, and from my reading, often petty. Like, really petty. I try to put those into one section to separate them from what I consider the historically important ones. The last three sections deal with the Covenant, the Constitution, and finally the Commonwealth, issues he inserted himself right into the middle of.

Dad was vehemently against approving the Covenant. He saw himself as a Micronesian, and wanted to remain a citizen of the nascent Micronesian nation. He did not want to give up his identify and the sovereignty of his people to become a powerless minority within the much larger American family.

Anyone with a passing knowledge of the Marianas knows he lost that battle. So as not to be excluded from the forming of the new government, he ran as a delegate to the first Northern Mariana Islands Constitutional Convention and won. He would later run for a seat in the Senate and lose.

My mother tells me that many of his letters were written while sitting at his desk in his law office, crafting his arguments on endless reams of yellow legal pads. In these letters he writes about historical events from the founding of the Commonwealth from a perspective that is increasingly forgotten in the Marianas today.

He made a lot of predictions in his writings. Some of what he wrote has come true, some has not. One important insight I gleamed from his letters is that our people have forgotten that we are culturally and geographically part of Micronesia, even if we are temporarily controlled by the United States. The decolonize movement has barely reached the shores of the Northern Marianas, but it is growing. There are American citizens living in our islands who think it is un-American for America to have colonies in the 21st Century. I hope that these letters will speak to those people, and provide historical context for how the unique relationship between the Commonwealth and the United States developed.

I wish my Dad were around today to talk to us about these things, but he's not. These letters are the next best thing.

Angelo O'Connor Villagomez
May 10, 2018

1 HAFA GACHONG

October 3, 1975
It feels good to be back on Saipan after three years of law school in Washington, D.C. Washington could be a great place to go to school. It is a highly intellectual city, generally speaking. It has high quality schools and as the nation's capital there is political, economic, and social excitement going on practically at all times. Students have the opportunity to keep up with the current events in the nation and the rest of the world.

As a Micronesian student, I encountered the so-called, "typical Micronesian student problems." I had to adjust to the food, the traffic jam, the crowded buses and restaurants and so forth. One very hard adjustment I had to make was the indifference that people showed to other people. These all add up to something called, "being homesick," but one can adjust to that also.

In the classroom I was confronted with the common language problem. Legal language is difficult enough for smart American law students. For an ordinary Micronesian student it is more than difficult, it is torture.

Now that I have graduated and returned I hope to participate in working on some of our island problems. In the public defender's office where I work, one of our duties is to help protect the fundamental rights of our citizens and also to help keep our public safety department from abusing its authority.

This column will appear weekly in this paper. It will contain my personal views on any given subject relevant to Micronesia. I will encourage and appreciate any response from the readers.

Asta i otro simana.

2 INDIAN LAW PROGRAM

September 1, 1972

Please allow me to convey this message to prospective Micronesian law students and the Trust Territory Government concerning a law school program which John Tarkong from Palau and myself attended this summer.

It is called "Indian Law Program" and is similar to a regular summer law school. It is established to prepare prospective Indian law students for law school and is held every summer for eight weeks at the University of New Mexico, school of law.

We were the first Micronesians allowed to participate in this program at our scholarship expenses and we found it absolutely helpful and effective in preparing students for law school. It introduces to the students the very basic and essential elements necessary for success in the study of law.

I urge every Micronesian, entering law school, to attend this program not only because of its preparatory effectiveness, but because it is also greatly educational studying with Indian students. I further suggest to the Trust Territory Government that it be more aware and concern over the legal minded Micronesians and encourage them to pursue a legal education through inspiration and assistance.

This program can be utilized for that purpose. It is not only prepares and encourages ambitious students; it also discourages and reveals non-ambitious students at an early non-critical stage and at a cheaper cost.

3 AFS SCHOLARSHIP

October 12, 1973
Please allow me to convey the following message to the public.

In the fall of 1967, the American Field Services International Scholarship Program (AFS) extended its hand to Micronesia. Since then, approximately eight Micronesian high school students are sent to attend one year of high school in the U.S. every year under AFS.

These students normally come from among the best students in different high schools in Micronesia. Over 90% of them successfully complete their studies in the U.S. and over 90% of them enter college after returning to Micronesia. They also seem to be more successful in college than Micronesians not participant in this program. However, there are exceptions to this general conclusion. Participants in the first AFS group have all graduated from college and are working in Micronesia. No doubt, the AFS program benefits Micronesia in a very crucial way. It borrows the best young brains from Micronesia and puts them through a year of cultural SHOCK in the U.S. This results in the enhancement of the students' educational interest and capabilities. Thus, it generally promotes educational and leadership growth in Micronesia.

The AFS does not only bring 3,000 students into the U.S. from 78 different countries per year, it also sends some American students to attend high school in the participating countries.

There is a definite plan to bring American high school students to Micronesia under this program in the year 1974. Picked among many applicants, an American student will come here to attend school. But before he gets here, a Saipanese family needs to volunteer to sponsor him/her. Normally, a family with a boy/girl the age of the American boy/girl is preferred. The family is urged to consider its new member as their own child for purposes of support, guidance, responsibility demands, etc. If the student and the family find it very difficult to communicate or be together, the student may be transferred to another family.

What this program does is it promotes racial and cultural interaction, understanding and acceptance throughout the world. And this is done through community and institutional efforts and cooperation. It is an AFS practice to have a community chapter whose duty is to ascertain the student's general needs for safety, comfort and health.

The T.T. Headquarters Scholarship office is a good source of information about the AFS. I urge families, teachers, students, public officials, and others to think about this program and what it does for our society. I certainly urge all students to try and get in this program. And I will suggest to families who apply to sponsor an American student that they will learn much about being an American and being a Saipanese. It will be a worthwhile experience.

The fact that I mention students coming to Saipan only does not mean that the other districts will not participate.

In case you are wondering, I learned about the AFS by going to high school in Wisconsin under it. It is the greatest program I have been attached to and it sparked my incentive to become what I am now, a law student.

4 GRADUATE SCHOOL SCHOLARSHIPS

July 12, 1974

This is an open letter to the Municipal Council, the Mayor, and Municipal Scholarship Board. I am writing with respect to the municipal ordinance which limits the eligibility for municipal scholarship assistance to undergraduate college students only. The ordinance expressly precludes assistance to graduate students.

Council members have expressed the following reasons for the ordinance.

1. A graduate student can make it better on his own.
2. An undergraduate needs more encouragement and assistance.
3. Saipan is in greater demand for undergraduates than for graduates.

It is understandable that because very few, if any, of our council members have been graduate students, they lacked the experience to know the practicability of this ordinance. However, they could have found out if they wanted to.

Let us be informed that it is three times more difficult to be a graduate student than to be an undergraduate student. The demands of undergraduate school are "peanuts" compared to graduate school. Many people quit graduate school because of its difficultly, but most people quit undergraduate school because they get bored. In addition, graduate school cost a hell of a lot more. It is therefore incorrect to presume that a graduate student can make it better on his own and that an undergraduate needs more encouragement and assistance.

It is not only incorrect, but ridiculous and stupid, to presume that Saipan is in greater demand for undergraduates than graduates. To be honest with ourselves, let us humbly accept the fact that undergraduates are generally lacking any productive skills. We need doctors, we need engineers, we need architects, psychiatrists, economists, CPA's, Lawyers, etc. Undergraduates are not even half way to obtaining these professions.

Let us therefore realize that we need to assist and encourage our graduate students just as much, if not more; and that this ordinance is harmful to our educational, economic, and social developments. Therefore, it must be amended to include the graduate students under eligibility. I request the newly elected members of the Council to take this initiative.

5 IMMIGRATION TROUBLES

October 4, 1974

For the benefit of Micronesian students going to school in the mainland, allow me to reveal my experiences with the U.S. immigration on Guam and Hawaii. But first, let me state two facts: 1) a Micronesian is required to obtain an immigration form (I-20), issued by the school, before entering the U.S. as a student, 2) if she enters without an I-20, she'll be admitted as a visitor but may subsequently change her status to that of a student upon application to the U.S. immigration and payment of $25.00.

In 1973, my I-20 did not arrive from school until after entering Guam as a visitor. Therefore, I paid my I-20 when I entered Guam. However, the immigration admitted me as a visitor, saying that I could only enter as a student in Hawaii. When I arrived in Hawaii, the immigration said I should have entered as a student on Guam and he would not admit me as a student. Therefore, I had to apply to change my status and had to pay $25.00.

To prevent these problems, students may do the following: 1) request for an I-20 four weeks in advance so you'll have it before entering the U.S. 2) If you have an I-20, make sure that you enter Guam as a student unless you are entering the U.S. through Hawaii first via Majuro.

The burden that is put upon Micronesian students by the U.S.

immigration is against the obligation and promise of the U.S. as an administering authority. The Trusteeship Agreement provides that the U.S. promises to promote education in Micronesia and encourage Micronesians seeking higher education. In that respect the U.S. should open the doors of its educational institutions and encourage Micronesians to enter easily without obstruction by the immigration or other government agencies. This would not be necessary, of course, if within the 27 years of its administration, the U.S. had built a university, which the Russian government says is long overdue in Micronesia.

6 SHAKESPEARE

May 19, 1972
Please allow me to answer a letter written by Mr. Oscar C. Rasa and Mr. Joaquin P. Villanueva to the people of the Marianas District. The letter was released through the May 5th issue of the Marianas Variety News Views on Saipan. Near the end, Mr. Rasa and Mr. Villanueva jointly wrote, "I ask each and every one of you to objectively scrutinize the merits and demerits of our statements." My comments are intended to encourage that certain statements and allegations be supported, explained or verified by Mr. Rasa and Mr. Villanueva. Their statements were so opinionated, general, and unsupported by facts that they could have been written by anybody who wanted to sound big.

Consider this statement, "we strongly believe that we do possess the highest credentials necessary to qualify for public servants." Of all the people in the Marianas, Mr. Rasa and Mr. Villanueva claim to have the highest credentials. OK, but as a voting citizen, I would like to know what these credentials are; how many years of public services have they rendered; what were their previous superb accomplishments in public services and so forth. Here is another one, "With enthusiasm and despair we have consistently witnessed the withering away of rational and effective leadership as evidenced by previous action on various crucial occasions. This is an outright challenge of the qualifications and accomplishments of the previous and present leaders of the Marianas District. Again, what did these leaders do or did not do? What was the particular issue or occasion and what would Mr. Rasa and Mr. Villanueva have done had they been in charge.

Mr. Rasa and Mr. Villanueva claim to have "high level of rational and cognitive competence - - a capacity for achievement, objectivity, fairness, and detachment, and ability to deal with high level abstractions and complex situations…extraordinary mentality…" When they wrote, "We declare our unquestionable possession of this ingredient." I don't mind the flowery words, they are beautiful, but I would like to see their claims and statements supported by facts, instances, and products.

There are few other things I would like to have clarified, but I will jump to the statement that says, "Above all these matters, we hold the highest qualifications to serve you because we do care for you and we want to help you and your children." Well, that would be like if the High Commissioner says, "I will pay every citizen a minimum of $5.00 an hour, pave every road and improve all public facilities because I like you people and I care for you." Is it really your feelings toward the people that give you your qualifications and capability? Of course not.

Frankly, about 90% of the "dear people of the Marianas District" would not comprehend or understand Mr. Rasa and Mr. Villanueva's letter because it was written in the language of Shakespeare. If their intention was to communicate to the people of the Marianas, they certainly have wasted every effort and the payment for the advertisement.

7 LEARN OR LEAVE

December 12, 1972
The letter written by Mr. Joe Mafnas to Mr. Arthur Akina and Luther
Baker deserves an answer from Mr. Akina and Mr. Baker.

Calling Micronesian "untrainable savages, monkeys, and niggers"
when dealing with a congressional representative must be explained
and justified by the speaker. In fact, it should not be said or it should
be explained under any circumstances.

The issue is very touchy and very emotional. It provokes hateful and
ill attitudes towards the Americans in Micronesia and even to the
administration. I regret that the speaker or speakers of these
distasteful words do not know better.

I too, feel that they should either learn or leave.

8 FOREIGN COLLUSION

November 22, 1974

I am shocked to know the popular party's so called "leaders" have been begging money from Japanese businessmen to finance their political campaigns. You know what that means? It means that if these beggars get elected, they will work more for the benefits of the Japanese businessmen than for the Marianas people. In other words, they would not be our true leaders and representatives. Instead they would be puppets of the friendly Japanese yen seekers. Isn't that disgusting? It's our blessing that they lost the election! Our Japanese Mayor Sablan ought to be ashamed for writing the beggar's letter, but maybe he doesn't know how to be ashamed.

In the U.S. such practice could be a crime under Chapter 8, Title 2 of the U.S. Code. Let us not make the same mistake again. No businessman gives away money for nothing in return.

9 OUR FULL-TIME DISTRICT LEGISLATURE

October 31, 1975

We have heard enough criticisms and remarks about our full-time District Legislature which are not nice. We have heard remarks that some of them do nothing but read the newspapers. We have also heard that some of them spend most of their time driving around the island or sitting around shooting the breeze. These may all be true, but certainly it cannot be true of all our legislators and for any legislator it cannot be true all the time.

We are not to compare our legislators with members of the U.S. Congress. Our legislature has just been made a full-time working body. They need time to develop their skills and experiences.

Certainly this is not to discourage our citizens from examining or criticizing their leaders. As we all know, our citizens have the right to do that and it is healthy for them to do it. After all, our citizens probably do think about the $8,000.00 that each of the sixteen legislators are earning per year. They naturally would not want to pay anybody $8,000.00 to read the newspaper.

On the other hand, we cannot realistically expect a perfect legislature. Instead we should expect that they will make mistakes and they have. For example, they have enacted legislations which were probably not well researched, studied or drafted. Specifically there was the bill to create a $2.25 minimum wage; the bill to require a 5-year residency of other T.T. citizens before they could vote in the Marianas; and the bill to require the private business sector to provide annual leave and sick leave for all employees without any exception. Legislations of these natures need to be studied to determine their impact on our economy or their constitutionality.

Naturally some people blame the situation on the legislative counsel. It is true that the legislators depend heavily upon their legislative counsels and they should be very careful and very choosy in their hiring of counsels. However, no one single person should be blamed. The problem is inevitable at this stage of our early development. We all had to trip and tumble before we learned to walk.

10 OUR DISTRICT LEGISLATURE IS BROKE

December 12, 1975

According to Honorable Larry Guerrero, our legislature has a deficit of $300,000. That's cool! We made it a full-time body and in a matter of months it goes broke. What better proof do we have of the type of leadership we have in this honorable institution. They have clearly demonstrated our readiness for self-government. They have demonstrated our ability to promote and sustain our economic progress. No doubt, with this type of progressive legislature our schools, hospitals and other institutions will rot and turn into soil. That's not bad, we'll have fertile land.

When the legislature passed a bill to create a minimum wage of $2.25 per hour, weren't we shocked? But certainly, nothing this honorable body does should surprise us anymore. Its PRESIDENT was taken into court and alleged to have embezzled $35,000 of the people's scarce money. What does that illustrate?

The same honorable body has passed legislation insidiously discriminating against the Carolinians in the election of delegates to the Constitutional Convention. It deprives them of their right to vote. Doesn't this body have a legal counsel? If not, it better get one quickly. Not only did it arbitrarily discriminate against certain classes, but it also set up a method of election which would ascertain the election of delegates having minimal or inadequate qualifications. That is, the method of election by at-large rather than by district.

It would be wise to place a minimal requirement of formal education on the delegates. For instance, it would be wise to require that a person have at least two years of college education to be delegate. Of course, the exceptions which are reasonable and practical may be allowed. If this is not done, our constitution to be, will probably be just as crazy as the bill creating the method of election discussed above.

I am not suggesting that there is no hope in the District Legislature. It has certainly accomplished many good deeds. There are certainly members with high qualities or potentials. But when they do flop, it is good and healthy for the public to know about it and talk about it. This is a fundamental element of democracy. It is an element of democracy which our District Legislature begged for when it begged for a U.S. commonwealth status.

11 WAR REPARATIONS

December 24, 1975
During World War II the Japanese fortified the islands of the Pacific Paradise, called Micronesia, and prepared her attack against Uncle Sam. Uncle Sam on the other hand, in order to defend his own territory returned the attack against Japan. That attack was made within our territory over and around our peaceful little islands. Our innocent citizens were killed, their homes and farms were destroyed. They became destitute by virtue of the Great Powers fighting for God knows what reason. They were not compensated then, but were promised compensation.

Today, over thirty years later, the two great fighters decided to compensate us. They may not have the legal duty, but they certainly have the moral obligation to do so. These two powers have been trustees for us. We have been beneficiaries. But instead of protecting us, they destroy us.

The people of Micronesia are dissatisfied with the war claims compensation for good reasons. The Claims Commission has grossly unfair rules and methods of determining damages. In death claims, the Commission sets the value of the dead person solely on his age at the time of death. It does not consider his health, the number of his children, his occupation, education, and so forth. The lack of such considerations is not only unfair, it is also contrary to Trust Territory law and International law.

The Commission determines damages to property based on the value of the dollar in 1944. That is ridiculous. Our losses did not terminate in 1944. They have continued until today and we are entitled to compensation for accumulated interest and inflation. Had we been paid in 1944, we would definitely receive such interest over the years.

After the Commission has unfairly determined the total damages, by regulation the claimant is entitled to receive only 16% of that amount. In the end, the claimant would receive approximately one percent (1%) of his actual loss.

We have been cheated and insulted. When the U.S. and Japan decide to fulfill their moral obligation to compensate, they should compensate 100% or close thereto. Otherwise, the compensation would not be worth the aggravation and frustration that it would provoke among our innocently victimized citizens.

Nevertheless, may the Great Powers and the people of Micronesia have a Merry Christmas and a Happy New Year.

12 IN DEFENSE OF FATHER JOE

January 16, 1976
I was totally shocked when I learned that 38 citizens of Saipan petitioned His Excellency, Bishop Flores of Guam to have Father Jose Villagomez of Saipan transferred. They did not say where he should be transferred to or why. All they said was that, "his behavior is discussed and criticized," and that he unnecessarily used language unbecoming of his profession."

These are totally inadequate reasons for petitioning that Father Villagomez be transferred from Saipan. The petition was submitted on August 21, 1975, but Father Villagomez has not been transferred. It is very unlikely that he would be transferred merely because 38 persons submitted such inadequate allegations. The following persons were the petitioners:

1. Lorenzo Tudela Camacho
2. Jose Ch. Camacho
3. Rita Sakisat Camacho
4. Magdalena C. Santos
5. Jose Naputi Santos
6. Lorenzo C. Pangelinan
7. Trinidad Camacho Kisa
8. Victoria Ch. Camacho
9. Maria N. Aldan

10. David T. Aldan
11. Antonio Camacho Muna
12. Margarita Camacho Muna
13. Pedro Nakatsukasa
14. Juan L.G. Demapan
15. Magdela Tudela
16. Benita B. Cepeda
17. Luis C. Cepeda
18. Federica A. Naputi
19. Jesus Hocog
20. Pedro C. Dela Cruz
21. Teresita Sn. Alfao
22. Felix Kisa
23. Juana Takai
24. M. Kapileo
25. A. Taitano
26. Rosa Taitano
27. Gregorio Basa
28. Isabel Ch. Pangelinan
29. Cecilia S. Camacho
30. Jose Sakisat
31. Luis Demapan
32. Jose C. Lizama
33. David A. Indalecio
34. Remedio Nakatsukasa
35. Albert P. Lizama
36. J. Mendiola
37. Daniel Quitugua
38. (Unreadable)

There is a rumor that the person who drafted the petition was Vicente N. Santos, President of the District Legislature. Let me emphasize that this is a rumor, even though most rumors on this island are reliable information.

If three or four thousand people sign such a petition, it would have some weight. Obviously, the petition as it was is groundless and fruitless. Certain of the above listed persons have apologized to His Excellency, Bishop Flores and to Father Villagomez.

Because this is a public document, I feel such a thing as this should be exposed publically, to prevent, in the future, such a petition.

13 RESIGNATIONS

April 2, 1976
As we read this column, the High Commissioner, the Deputy High Commissioner, the Attorney General and several Department Heads are preparing to leave their positions and the Trust Territory, according to the Pacific Daily News. Some of them are resigning and some are being fired. We do not know all the facts and circumstances surrounding the resignations or firings but we can safely presume that there are good reasons for such happenings.

Some of us are happy about the situation and some of us are disappointed. However, it is too early to have any strong feelings about the resignations. If the persons resigning are to be replaced by Micronesians, I will be pleased and thankful to the United States. The time has passed when the Micronesians should hold the highest positions in their government. On the other hand, if the persons resigning are to be replaced by other Americans, I will be very disappointed.

The United States, upon its own initiative, took over responsibility for the development of Micronesia in its economic, educational, social and political affairs. It has had thirty years to do that. If, in thirty years, the U.S. has not been able to educate and train Micronesians to be able to govern themselves, then the U.S. has ignored its obligation and has failed as a trustee for the Micronesian people.

We hear that members of the District Legislature are asking the Secretary of the Interior to suspend or revoke the legislative election this November. Here is another clear example of the stupidity and misunderstanding of democracy that some of our leaders have shown. On the one hand, they scream, "We want democracy and we want to join the American family," and on the other hand, at the same time, they scream, "We don't want democratic procedures and elections. We want dictatorship." The question I raise is, what do they really want? They cannot have both. That's for sure!

14 PALAU'S RIGHT TO SELF-DETERMINATION

August 11, 1976

I have been in Washington, D.C. for two months where I studied and took the bar exam. That is the reason why this column has not appeared during the same period. Now that I have returned, I hope to continue writing for this good paper in this column. There were certain important events occurring during my absence about which I was anxious to write. However, my lack of time prevented me from doing so. Let me briefly touch on some of them now.

When former Ambassador H. Williams announced that Palau District may not enter into separate negotiations with the United States, I was totally shocked. The ambassador completely reversed his position on the issue of the people's right of self-determination. When the Marianas asked for separate negotiations, the ambassador was pleased. He was pleased because the Marianas was a separate district having a unique culture and a separate right of self-determination. But doesn't the ambassador realize that Palau is also a separate district, having its own unique culture and a separate right of self-determination? Of course he does. Nevertheless, the ambassador realized further that the right of self-determination for Micronesians is not inherent. It is a right that could be given to Micronesians by the U.S. if the U.S will benefit as a result. The ambassador concluded that the granting of the right of self-determination to Palau District would not be in the interest of the United States. Therefore, Palau does not have the same right that the Marianas has.

When the Marianas wanted to separate, the ambassador expressed that the U.S. supported fragmentation of Micronesia. When Palau wanted to separate, the ambassador expressed that the U.S. did not support fragmentation of Micronesia. Perhaps the ambassador is not being dishonest, but he cannot be telling the truth.

****

It is fascinating the way that the Marianas Legislature plays games with the resident commissioner over the ConCon Bill. The position of the rescom is more just and practical, and the legislature is wasting time, money and energy. No doubt, the situation is teaching us a great deal about "democracy" and "leadership." This is a difficult but a natural situation in a developing government as ours. However, let us pray that our legislature will continue to learn fast so that they will become more fruitful than wasteful.

****

It is pleasing to know that Speaker Vicente N. Santos wishes to settle his case with the T.T. Government for $8,000.00. At least he appears to be "honest" in admitting that he took money which he was not entitled to take. But more pleasing is the fact that the government is reluctant to settle for only $8,000.00. The government should be paid every penny that it was wrongfully deprived of. If the speaker refused to make complete payments, then the government should resort to the court of law.

15 THE CIRCUS

April 28, 1977
One day last week I was in the law library of the High Court when a person I knew came in. The first thing he said to me was "I hear that you are transferring to the Legislature?" I replied, "Yes, that is a probability." He then said to me, "How can you do that, that place is like a circus." At that point, I decide not to say anything further or to discuss the matter.

That person is indeed entitled to his opinion about our District Legislature, and he may strongly believe that our Legislature is like a circus. What that means is that our legislature consists of a bunch of fascinating clowns and animals whose purposes are merely to act funny and to make people laugh. We don't have a circus here in the Northern Marianas, but some of us who have been to the United States might have had the opportunity to see one, and those people will know better what that person thinks of our Legislature when he says it is like a circus.

I certainly disagree with him that we have a legislature which is like a circus. In addition, I disagree with him that a person should refrain from working with our legislature or that any person should be discouraged from working with our legislature simply because that person thinks that our legislature is like a circus. Our legislature is less than twenty-five years old unlike many states or local legislatures in the United States, some of which have been in existence for two hundred years. However, in comparing our legislature with similar types of legislatures in the United States local governments, I think that our legislature is equal if not more advanced in sophistication and academics. I am not saying that our legislature is superior to other legislatures, or that it does not need any improvement and that it cannot be criticized, but I do think that it is a long way from being like a circus.

Indeed any person may feel the way he wants to feel and may express his feelings in public as he deems proper, as long as he is not personally attacking and defaming or harming another person's reputation. At the same time, people should be responsible and should try to be as honest as possible in expressing their opinions and criticisms about people and the leadership of any particular society. For any outsider to come into the Northern Marianas and to make such disgraceful statements about our lawmaking body can be tolerated only if it is true and well-intended. Any person who does that should be prepared to answer to the particular group of people or leadership that he is labeling or making a mockery of indiscreetly. Our legislators now know what some of our friendly outsiders think of them. It is up to them to prove that they are or that they are not like a bunch of people put together like a circus.

I personally have criticized our legislature many times before and I have disagreed with many of the bills or resolutions they have enacted. This is proper and healthy. But to simply label our leadership body as a <u>CIRCUS</u> is beyond human integrity.

16 GARBAGE PAPER

September 8, 1977

Out of curiosity I glanced through the <u>Munchi Narara</u> for the first time this morning. I was disappointed that I spent ten cents on such a piece of garbage. That junk should not be put out where children could read it. It should be restricted to adult garbage readers only. The language used in that garbage paper is filthy and disgusting. For example, in describing an official of Continental Airlines, the garbage paper called this person "KATSAKA" which is the Chamorro equivalent of "COCK SUCKER." This is just one of the many examples of indecent language used in that garbage paper.

The content of the paper itself is probably worth half a penny. Rumor has it that the only purpose of the paper is to gratify the editor by seeing his picture in it. The paper it is printed on is worth about three pennies. If the paper were sold at five cents, it should make a great profit. But to sell such garbage at ten cents a copy is an unconscionable rip-off.

17 ELECTIONS

November 10, 1977

Permit me to discuss with the people of the Northern Marianas whether it is good or not to make a governor out of a rich person. I have heard a number of my brothers in the Democratic Party expressing the opinion that it is not good to vote for Joeten or Oly for governor and lt. governor because they are rich individuals.

After days and weeks of wrestling with this question I still cannot be satisfied that the opinion of my democratic brothers make any sense. I cannot see how being rich makes a person a bad candidate for a governor or lt. governor. On the other hand, we have great examples proving that rich persons have made excellent governors and presidents of the United States of America.

President Jimmy Carter is one of the richest men in America. He was a businessman and a millionaire and now a U.S president. Are we to say that President Carter, the President who approves our constitution, is a bad president because he is rich and was a businessman before becoming a president?

President John F. Kennedy whom we loved and whose memorial we implanted permanently in front of our Mt. Carmel church was one of the richest men in the whole world. He was in business and was a millionaire. Then he became a great U.S. president. Are we to say that President Kennedy was a bad President because he was rich? Are we to say that the American people are crazy because they vote for such rich individuals to be their presidents?

Governor Nelson Rockefeller of New York was one of the richest men in the world. Was he a bad governor because he is rich?

President Carter, Kennedy and Governor Rockefeller did not need their executive offices to improve their financial situations. When they were businessmen they did their best to promote their businesses and when they were presidents and governor, they did their best to promote the government interests and serve the people. Similarly, Joeten and Oly do not need the executive positions to improve their financial situations. When they are purely businessmen, they do their best to promote their businesses. But when they become governor and lt. governor, they will do their best to promote the government interests and serve our people.

Therefore, the statements that Joeten and Oly will not make good executives are misleading and irresponsible statements. Such statements have no foundation, no relevancy and are pure "BIRACK."

18 A LOVE LETTER TO MIKE WHITE

November 17, 1977
The Northern Marianas Legislature has prepared an amendment to the election law in order to clearly define the term "U.S. citizen or national." It will be defined to mean those persons in the Northern Marianas who, upon termination of the Trusteeship Agreement, will become U.S. citizens or nationals according to the Covenant. The amendment is signed and supported by a majority of the elected leaders in the legislature including democrats and territorials.

The intent of the amendment is to comply with the Constitution and the equal protection of the laws. That is, if the people of the Northern Marianas cannot vote or run for office in the U.S. because they are not U.S. citizens, then U.S. citizens should not be able to vote or run for office in the Northern Marianas because they are not included in the Covenant. This is clear proof that the elected leaders of the Northern Marianas still maintain the feeling of obligation to protect their people against any further exploitation and suppression. I for one cannot in good conscience accept the idea that Americans or anybody could have rights in our home while at the same time we the Chamorros and Carolinians could not have the same rights in their home. Law and logic dictate that this is unconstitutional and against the equal protection of the laws.

The effect of the amendment is that it will disqualify Mr. Mike White and any U.S. citizen from voting or running for office in the upcoming election until we become U.S. citizens.

We have inherited some funny campaign techniques which our brother, Mr. White, has brought to the Northern Marianas from Philadelphia. Mr. White told our people in a campaign speech that Ramon Villagomez told him to go back to his land. First of all, that is not true. I have never told that to anybody. But more important, how is such an untrue statement going to help a Philadelphian get elected in the Northern Marianas?

Mr. White also told our people that Ramon Villagomez likes American girls more than Chamorros girls because he is married to an American. However, he forgot to tell our people that Ramon was a student in the U.S. since he was 17 until he was 25 years old and did not have the "bionic" ability to court girls in Saipan. But more important, how does Ramon being married to an American relate to Mr. White's running for Congress? Is he running on the basis of who likes what kind of girls? He who marries a local girl is more qualified? I'm sorry but I have to laugh. Furthermore, how is a stupid statement like that going to help a Philadelphian get elected in the Northern Marianas? It is a Philadelphian style.

19 A LOVE LETTER TO CARLOS CAMACHO

January 10, 1978
Article II, Section 2, of the Northern Marianas Constitution states in part that, "The governor shall be…a resident and domiciliary of the Commonwealth for at least seven years immediately preceeding the date on which the governor takes office." In explaining this section and declaring the intent of the Constitution, the Analysis of the Constitution states on page 60 that, "Residency means that place currently inhabited by the person, <u>regardless of intention to remain in the future</u>." (emphasis added)

Under the above section of our Constitution Dr. Carlos S. Camacho is not qualified to take office as governor on January 9, 1978. In 1972, Dr. Camacho was in Hawaii studying for a Master's Degree for over a year. Therefore, he was not residing in the Northern Marianas. He has not been residing in the Northern Marianas for seven years immediately preceding January 9, 1978, thus he is ineligible to take office.

If Dr. Camacho is allowed to take office, then the people of the Northern Marianas will have a governor who is ineligible and who is an unconstitutional governor. His governorship will be in violation of the constitution and therefore should be null and void.

Why the Election Board certified a person who is ineligible is beyond my legal comprehension. The act of the board is also in violation of the Constitution and is legally null and void.

The result of all this is that we have an unconstitutional government based on a worthless and meaningless constitution. We have started on the wrong step. God only knows where the following steps will fall.

20 A LOVE LETTER TO CISCO ULUDONG

February 23, 1979
There is an article in the Pacific Daily News, February 18, 1979, regarding the death of Jack Mouncier written by Cisco Uludong (PDN reporter on Saipan). The article in its entirety is incorrect, untrue, and is fabricated.

To begin with, the article is entitled, "Murder Case Moved to Lower Court." This statement is wrong in that there has been no murder case with respect to the death of Jack Mouncier and no such case has been moved to a lower court. The article then states that the murder case has been transferred from the Federal District Court to the Commonwealth Trial Court. That statement is incorrect and untrue in that there has been no murder case transferred from the Federal District Court to the Commonwealth Trial Court in relation to the death of Jack Mouncier.

The article continues to state that under the Commonwealth Constitution, juvenile cases are tried in the Commonwealth Trial Court. This is also not correct in that nothing in the Constitution provides for juvenile cases being tried in the Commonwealth Trial Court. The statement that, "Federal Judge Alfred Laureta ordered the case moved to the lower court," is incorrect in that there has been no such order by Judge Laureta. Furthermore, the Commonwealth Trial Court is not a "lower court" in relation to the

Federal District Court sitting as a local court in the Northern Marianas.

The article states that a sixteen year old has been accused of the stabbing murder three weeks ago. That statement is not true in that there has been no murder charges in connection with the death of Mouncier and there has been no finding by any court that there was such a murder. Furthermore, the article states that Laureta has issued a "gag order" to all parties involved. That statement is not true in that there has been no such order by Judge Laureta.

Finally, the article states that Herb Soll, the new judge will hear the case before a decision is made on the youth's status. That statement is also untrue in that no case has been filed with the Commonwealth Trial Court and that there has been no transfer of the case from the Federal District Court.

The article is ridiculous, untrue and clearly illustrative of the reporter's irresponsibility and stupidity.

21 THE SPIRIT OF QUEEN MARIANA

September 14, 1973
It appears from the report of the last Marianas Political Status Negotiation that the Marianas is taking a strong position not to sell Tinian to the U.S. War Department. The U.S. takes the position that it does not lease, it buys. Therefore, it should buy Tinian.

The Marianas has the bargaining power and the legal protection not to sell Tinian if it deems it not to be in the best interest of its people. It is a very wise decision not to sell Tinian and the Marianas team ought to stick to that position.

I hope to the spirit of the late Queen Mariana that our good legendary neighbor, honorable Taga, will not forever be doomed into the hands of the warheads.

This good and valuable territory should not be sold and if leased, it shouldn't be leased for as long as 99 years. Even the forefathers of our infant society cannot project into such distant future.

The Chamorros of our tiny islands, being of sound mind, realize that they cannot afford to forever release their BEST lands to the richest and most powerful warriors in this world, and to keep for themselves the hills and the rocks, upon which to produce their taro and build their integrity. We are not rich and we are not powerful, but we have means to protect our lands, our unique and small society, and our future.

22 A LETTER TO THE HIGH COMMISSIONER

November 22, 1973
The act of the High Commissioner in vetoing the Micronesian Legal Services budget proposal is outrageous. It is abusive of his executory power. Here is a very clear example of an American government representative – a guardian – suppressing and condemning the true and wholesome interests of his wards, the Micronesian people and their true native leaders.

As between the American representative in Micronesia, Edward E. Johnston, and the people of Micronesia, there exists a revolting struggle as a result of two conflicting interests between them.

It appears very clearly from the apparent set of circumstances that the interest of the American government in Micronesia, represented by Edward E. Johnston, is to preclude and eliminate any means by which the Micronesian people may challenge or object to a corrupt and suppressive American Administration in Micronesia.

It is the wholesome interest of the Micronesian people on the other hand, to obtain and keep any means by which they can justifiably and judicially challenge any corruption, suppression, or deficiency in the American Administration in their own home in Micronesia.

We, the "underdeveloped" Micronesians or wards did not learn about our fundamental rights to challenge the administration from the Spanish or the Germans or the Japanese. We learned it from the Americans and the American Constitution.

Edward E. Johnston must have pledged to uphold the Constitution of the United States when he was sworn into his present office. I doubt that "he pledged to deny the Micronesian people the same fundamental rights that are given the American people not only by their great Constitution, but also their Declaration of Independence.

It is my proposition that the act of the High Commissioner in vetoing the MLSC budget is contrary to his oath; it is contrary to the constitution of the United States which he has the duty to uphold; it is contrary to the purposes for which his office was created; and it is contrary or a denial of a fundamental right of the Micronesian people.

I therefore think it necessary, that in the interest of settling this conflict; in the interest of protecting the rights of the Micronesian people, and in the interest of implementing the true purposes and responsibilities of the United States Government in Micronesia, Edward E. Johnston, High Commissioner of the Trust Territory of the Pacific Islands Micronesia, ought to be "impeached."

23 A QUESTION FOR TINIAN

November 30, 1973

This letter is intended for the people of Tinian mainly but it relates to the people of Saipan too. May I ask the people of Tinian to think very seriously about the attempted rape that occurred on their peaceful island a week or so ago; the attempted rape done by the American Navy man among those warmly invited and kindly treated to island hospitality. And as you think about it, ask yourselves the following questions. (1) Do you really trust the U.S. military men? (2) How many U.S. military men will you have on your island when 2/3 of it is taken over by them? I would suggest that 10 to 20 thousand is quite conceivable. (3) Do you really know what kind of trouble you are asking for when you ask for the U.S. Military?

There is a serious lesson for us to learn from this revolting incident. We are not to let it pass and shut our eyes to it. We must think about it, talk about it, get sick about it, and do something about it. Do anything to prevent rapists roaming around and inside our homes. Thanks to the Navy, we are being warned.

24 DIVIDE AND CONQUER

January 25, 1974
After years and years of arduous research, I finally discovered the most effective political strategy that may win the United States the greatest victory over Micronesia. Ambassador Williams and his team deserve to learn this complex but indispensable method. It goes as follows:

"DIVIDE AND CONQUER"

If the U.S. negotiators avoid this strategy, they'll be making a mistake which is good for Micronesia. Those of us who are indifferent, let's sit back and watch. And as we watch, let's count as follows:

"one down"

"two down"

"three down"

"three to go"

25 SO-CALLED "LEADERSHIP"

November 11, 1974

In the midst of all the confusion about what the future of the Marianas should be, what commonwealth means and why we still negotiate when our chief negotiator, Edward Pangelinan, says he does not know what he is negotiating for, we could still be optimistic because we have people who would stand and fight for our rights to decide our own future, our rights to our land, our rights to develop our capabilities and our rights to govern ourselves. We are tired of being ordered by outsiders what to do and what not to do. We are tired of being deprived of our land and it looks like we are about to lose three-fourths of Tinian, one fifth of Saipan and a northern island. We are tired of outsiders deciding for us who could build a hotel on our Micro Beach, when homesteading would stop on Tinian, what laws should govern us, and most of all, we are sick of being enticed to believe the fiction that, in order to gain a better life we must become citizens of another country, particularly the United States.

We must learn to recognize persons in our community who have shown to have the qualifications and have made the commitment to represent our people and lead us in the direction that would develop our own identify and our ability to govern ourselves, promote our own welfare and protect our own interests.

Long before becoming a member of the Marianas Political Status Commission and chairman of its Land Committee, Pedro A. Tenorio, publicly expressed grave concern over the type of so-called "leadership" we have in the Marianas and the extent to which the rights and interests of our people are represented and protected. First, he raised issues concerning the land transactions on Tinian involving members of the Commission and other so-called "leaders" immediately after the U.S. revealed her desire to purchase Tinian. Second, he expressed grave concern over the alleged misuse of the District Legislature's fund. Subsequently, Mr. Tenorio joined the Status Commission and a few weeks ago we read in the Marianas Variety about his trip to Washington, DC to negotiate a lease over land on Tinian and Saipan. Although we do not know the full context of that negotiation, we are aware that no agreement was concluded because the U.S. offered an unreasonably low price. And our representative, Mr. Tenorio, persistently demanded that he knew what was fair for his people and did not agree to anything short of his proper representation of the rights of his people. (The next logical thing we will discover is that the U.S. would be trying to get Mr. Tenorio out of the Commission or the land committee.)

The point is, however, that Mr. Tenorio abhors dishonesty within our so-called "leadership." He has demonstrated the ability to adequately represent the true interests of his people. Mr. Tenorio will not bow to the unfair demands of the "outside world," he will communicate and listen to our problems, and we will be wise to cooperate and support him in his efforts to help us.

26 SLOW DOWN

January 3, 1975
This is an open letter to our newly elected Senator Pete Tenorio.

Senator Tenorio, I've heard that you are being accused of slowing down the Marianas negotiations. I want you to know that I envy your position. The people of the Marianas want you to be careful and slow down in drafting the Covenant which will determine our lives tomorrow. The rest of Micronesia wants you to do likewise. Most people in the U.S. that I have talked to also wish that you would take it slowly, carefully, and intelligently. May our prayers enlighten the other members of the Commission to also be slow, cautious and thorough in their evaluation of the agreements to be entered.

27 LAND ACQUISITION

January 31, 1975
The people of Micronesia and particularly the Marianas should be made to understand that under American foreign policy, Ambassador Williams has an obligation to represent with due diligence the best interest of the United States in seeking to obtain lands in Micronesia for military purposes. Therefore, Williams is not going to be as sympathetic to the rights and needs of the Micronesian people as we would like for him to be and as the United States has promised the WORLD by way of the trusteeship agreement with the United Nations.

There is a definite conflict of interest here on the part of the United States. On the one hand, the U.S. pledged to protect us, Micronesians, from the loss of our lands for its own use. Now the practical question is, would the U.S. sacrifice its land needs in Micronesia in order to fulfill its obligations under the trusteeship agreement? The obvious answer is, NO! The U.S. is obviously undertaking a breach of its agreement in order to promote its own interests in Micronesia – land acquisition.

The U.S. has made the breach primarily by acquiescing to the illegally created Marianas Political Status Commission and the illegal separate movement of the Marianas under international law since the movement is based on the principle of self-determination. Even after the U.S. has expressly given our Congress of Micronesia the power to all rightful subjects of legislation, it refuses to recognize that power by bypassing the Joint Political Status Committee which has the exclusive power, delegated by Congress, to negotiate with the U.S. on behalf of Micronesia. This illustrates clearly how honest and sympathetic the United States of America is with regard to its foreign policy in Micronesia.

The next practical question is, why are the Micronesian people <u>not in court</u> to challenge the acts of the U.S. and the Marianas?

28 HOGWASH

February 7, 1975
Please allow me to communicate this letter to my fellow citizens of
the Marianas.

I hereby cast my vote AGAINST the "covenant" for the
Commonwealth of the Northern Marianas!!

I have read the covenant several times. It is a disgusting document if
one is a citizen of the Marianas and can read and understand the legal
implications of the numerous double-talks in the covenant. On the
other hand, the document must sound very promising if one were an
American negotiator.

Under the covenant, the Marianas government structure and judicial
system are established. Therefore, we will be wasting our time to
draft the so-called, "your own" constitution. Besides, our
constitution will be inferior to the U.S. constitution, treaties, and
federal laws. The U.S. Congress, under the covenant, will have
absolute control over everything pertaining to the Marianas.
Therefore, we are being <u>fools</u> to think that we will have any form of
"self-government" under this covenant.

Under the covenant the U.S. will have absolute sovereignty and power of eminent domain in the Marianas. That means that the U.S. can and most likely will take all the land it wants in the Marianas.

The U.S. will lease 11,738 acres of our best lands for 100 years at $10.74 per acre per year plus 6,444 acres for $9.74 per acre per year. Our land is definitely not that cheap! The U.S. guarantees $14 million per year for only SEVEN years to support our funds. After the SEVEN years, we can all go sink our heads in the sand.

The covenant also provides that we can choose to either be American citizens or nationals, but the nationals will not have as many privileges as the citizens. That seems violative of the equal protection laws.

Under the covenant we will be stuck permanently and will never again be able to negotiate with anybody in the world. Do we want that for our children?

If the Marianas Political Status Commission thinks it has created an agreement to promote and protect the best interest of the people of the Marianas, then its members are a bunch of fools. They have spent about $100,000 on lawyers and what legal advice did they obtain? HOGWASH! Legal Services would have provided a million times better legal advice.

I urge all you fellow Marianas citizens, friends and relatives to vote against the document until they improve it, translate it to Chamorro and perhaps Carolinian and have it read to the people.

I urge all of Micronesia to petition the United Nations to conduct the plebiscite for Micronesia and the Marianas in order to protect our voters from outside interference. This has been the U.S. practice in terminating other trust territories.

29 ABSOLUTE SOVEREIGNTY

February 15, 1975

The greatest Pacific rip-off is about to happen. The U.S. is about to buy land in Micronesia (its own trust territory) for an average of $1,074 per acre; approximately $30,000 less than what the land is worth per acre.

However, the transaction will not be called a sale. It will be called a lease "for a term of 50 years" with "the option of renewing this lease…for an additional term of 50 years…" The U.S. will pay $19,520,600.00 for 18,182 acres "in full settlement of this lease, <u>including the renewal option</u>…"

The lease will be executed through a "covenant" which will create the U.S. commonwealth of the Northern Marianas, legally identical to a territory. Under the covenant the U.S. will also acquire absolute sovereignty and power of eminent domain over the Marianas. Thus the U.S. will also be buying the people and control over their government.

With these powers the U.S. could make the lease permanent. Therefore, for all practical purposes the lease is actually a sale. In addition, the U.S. could take additional land through eminent domain.

It is hard to understand why the Marianas citizens would sell their lives and their future. Nor is it easy to understand why they would sell their land at $1,074.00 per acre when it is worth $31,000.00 per acre. But one can certainly conclude that the Marianas people are being tricked.

An annoying thing is that the U.S. trustee for the Micronesian people has pledged to protect the islanders from the loss of their lands and resources, yet the U.S. is the one that would rip-off their land. This is contrary to the statement of President Ford when he said, "Honestly is the glue that holds the government together." I agree with President Ford, and the U.S. should reconsider its policies in Micronesia.

30 DESTROYING THE MICRONESIAN NATION

The signing of the "covenant" does not mean that the Northern Marianas are sold. The people who signed the covenant are sold, but the people of the Marianas are not. The signing of the covenant signifies only that the majority of the Marianas negotiators have agreed to stop negotiating. They have exhausted the minimum effort they could exert to protect their people and their children.

The signed covenant has no legal effect now or even after the Marianas District Legislature approves it. It also will have no legal effect after the majority of the Marianas voters vote in favor of the covenant.

If the covenant is not translated into Chamorro and if the people of the Marianas do not understand the contents of the covenant, I predict that they <u>will not</u> vote in favor of the covenant. I have not read the signed covenant, but I will cast my vote as soon as I have read it 2 or 3 times carefully. I urge my fellow Marianas citizens to <u>read</u> and <u>understand</u> the covenant before voting for or against it.

The Trust Territory high court denied a restraining order against the signing of the covenant. That is of course expected from such a court. We cannot expect the T.T. high court to rule against the national interest of the United States. It does not have the political authority to do that. The T.T. high court has only the power to adjudicate local matters and it cannot rule against the United States. That is why the <u>continental case</u> could not be resolved in the T.T. high court.

However, the Micronesians can assert their claims against the U.S. in the U.S. federal courts. This is the perfect time for the Congress of Micronesia to challenge the propriety of the Marianas separate political movement. The Marianas Political Status Commission (MPSC) is an illegally created body and that question needs to be resolved in the federal courts. The question whether the MPSC is an illegal entity is not a political question, as the MPSC argues. It is a justiciable legal question which is proper for the federal courts to decide.

There is no more time to wait. The Congress has the <u>duty</u> to protect Micronesia and it must act now. This is the time for all Micronesia to challenge the United States' efforts in destroying the Micronesian evolving nation. The Congress <u>can</u> and <u>must</u> prevent its own death

31 STATISTICS

March 14, 1975
Our of the estimated 14,500 people of the Marianas District of Micronesia, roughly 20 per cent or 3,000 are in favor of a commonwealth status for the Marianas. These 3,000 people constitute about one half of the total voting population of the Marianas. Statistics show that roughly 60 per cent or 8,500 of the people of the Marianas are below the age of 18, which is the voting age. However, these 30 per cent claim to represent the majority will of the people of the Marianas. Isn't that interesting?

This small minority of the Marianas citizens who claim to constitute the majority are well represented in the Congress of Micronesia. They hold a challenging vote of 3 per cent, which is one (1) senator out of the twelve (12) and zero (0) out of the twenty-one (21) representatives. Isn't that interesting, too?

32 TRUST THE PEOPLE

March 21, 1975
The people of the Marianas have been deprived of their democratic choice of leadership in their so-called "democratic government."

The Marianas leadership used to consist partially of former Senator Edward Pangelinan and former Congressman Herman Q. Guerrero of the Congress of Micronesia (COM). As members of the Joint Committee on Future Status (JCFS) of the COM, Pangelinan and Guerrero were automatically made members of the Marianas Political Status Commission (MPSC). Pangelinan and Guerrero were champions of the movement for commonwealth status.

However, in November, 1974, Guerrero and Pangelinan were democratically voted out of their seats and replaced by Senator Pedro Tenorio and Congressman Oscar Rasa. Tenorio and Rasa were new members of the JCFS and MPSC. THE PEOPLE ELECTED TO CHANGE THEIR LEADERSHIP FROM THOSE WHO FULLY SUPPORT COMMONWEALTH TO THOSE WHO DO NOT FULLY SUPPORT COMMONWEALTH. The election result was bottomed on that issue.

Nevertheless, through administrative maneuvers, Pangelinan was retained as member and chairman of the MPSC. Pangelinan was retained in an office from which the PEOPLE have ELECTED to throw him out.

The practice is undemocratic, it is un-American and it offends the integrity of the Marianas voters. If the people of the Marianas are to become Americans, they must be allowed to practice the American principle of democracy.

They must be allowed to have Senator Tenorio and Congressman Rasa as their TRUE leaders and the champions of their future political status.

Pangelinan has been democratically replaced by the people and the people must be afforded their choice of leadership.

33 POLITICAL MANEUVERS

April 4, 1975

Let the people of the Marianas be reminded that their district legislature has again engaged in an undemocratic, un-American and irresponsible political maneuver. In the U.S. such an act is unconstitutional.

The legislature passed a bill requiring that in order for residents of other districts to be eligible to vote in the Marianas the have to reside in the Marianas for at least five years. President Vicente Santos made it clear that the purpose of this bill is to prevent any political influence by Micronesians from other districts.

It is obvious that this whole question involves a political battle between the political parties. The popular party lost in the last election. The popular party leaders blamed their defeat on the residents of other districts voting in the Marianas. Thus they enacted this bill solely with the intention of defeating the territorial party. More specifically, the popular party wants to protect its political power for the upcoming plebiscite on the covenant for the commonwealth. Therefore, the bill is not intended for any public good.

This bill discriminates and deprives certain Micronesians of their fundamental rights to vote, their fundamental rights to travel and fundamental rights to equal protection of the laws.

Since this discriminatory bill is directed against the territorial party, this party has the duty to protect itself against an unjust and irrational political maneuver. Such a ridiculous law must be challenged in court by residents from other districts. A class action would be inevitable in this case.

34 AMERICAN WORKERS

April 11, 1975

In my recent conversations with the attorney for Ambassador Williams, I asked the following question: If the Marianas become a commonwealth under the present form of the covenant would the Marianas citizens be given jobs before other Americans are given the same jobs? His answer was, "No, if the other Americans are more qualified, they would be given the jobs first and the citizens of the Marianas would have to compete equally with any other Americans."

Now may we pose the following question to the people of the Marianas: Are you ready and willing to give up your jobs in the Marianas to Americans? Since the U.S. is overflowing with qualified people in every field and since millions of qualified Americans are desperately seeking jobs, it is realistic to think that thousands of Americans would come to the Marianas and take over jobs as soon as the Marianas becomes a commonwealth. Is that what the people of the Marianas want? If they say yes, then they have been misled. The people of the Marianas do not want to lose their jobs to other Americans. It appears that they even complain that many jobs in the Marianas are taken over by Filipinos, Koreans, other Micronesians and so forth.

If the jobs in the Marianas are taken over by other Americans, then the millions of dollars which the U.S. will pay to the Marianas will not go to the native citizens, it will go to the other Americans who would constitute the working citizens. The people of the Marianas should think about this seriously and they should vote against the covenant if they do not want to lose their jobs.

35 ONLY A NAME

April 25, 1975
Some people in the Marianas are confused as to the meaning of the word "covenant" and the meaning of the word "commonwealth." May I offer to explain.

"Covenant" is the document, signed by Ambassador Williams and ex-senator Edward Pangelinan, which contains the agreements between Williams and Pangelinan. It contains the land lease; it lists the U.S. laws that will apply in the Marianas; establishes the Marianas government system, its powers and obligations; and creates the administrative and judicial relationship between the U.S. national government and the Marianas as a <u>local</u> U.S. government.

"Commonwealth" is a different thing. It is simply a <u>name</u> which will be given to the government of the Marianas after the termination of the trusteeship agreement. Commonwealth simply means a government entity inferior to the U.S. national government. For instance, <u>Massachusetts</u> is officially called a <u>commonwealth</u>. But it is also a state and its government status is different from the Commonwealth of Puerto Rico and the Marianas. The main similarity is that they are all inferior to the U.S. national government.

From this we can reason that the name commonwealth is not important. What is important are the contents of the <u>covenant</u>. In addition, when one says that she is against the <u>covenant,</u> it does not follow that she is against commonwealth. The contents of the signed covenant could be changed 50% or more and we would still call the government under it a commonwealth.

The people of the Marianas can have a commonwealth without losing their land, their jobs, and without becoming victims of the evils of casino-gambling, corruption, strikes, crimes, and other imported headaches. They can do this by amending the signed covenant so as to contain agreements which would protect and promote the interests and welfare of the Marianas people today and tomorrow.

36 THANKS FOR THE LETTERS

May 2, 1975
I appreciate the letters in response to my letters to the editor with respect to the covenant. I wish more people would write about the covenant and not about who is bad and who is good. I also wish that Mr. Esteban J. Cepeda (whoever he is) would not again try to discourage our people from criticizing our government or any agency of our government. He should understand that it is healthy and sometimes necessary to criticize the government.

For instance, it is not important whether the Status Commission took two weeks or two years to draft the covenant. If the covenant is inadequate, we should criticize them. We do not bless an inadequate covenant just because it took two years to draft. But we should bless a good covenant even if it took two days to draft.

The American government is rich and powerful and mainly because the American people criticize their government. It was the critical Americans who rid the U.S. of the corrupted Vice President Agnew, President Nixon, Attorney General Mitchell, and a whole list of them.

It is typical for Micronesians to hesitate to criticize authority, but remember, we are not anymore under the Japanese military rule. We are almost under our own rule. Therefore, let us keep our leaders on their toes. Do not hesitate to criticize them when they turn their heads to the left and also when they turn their heads to the right. That way, they will keep their heads straight forward and their noses clean.

37 NOT INSANE

July 18, 1975

When Honorable Jose R. Cruz of Tinian made the statement that the Interior Secretary, Stanley Hathaway, was insane and did not know what he was talking about in his secretarial order, Joe was wrong. The Secretary of the Interior of the United States of America is <u>not insane</u>. He knew what he was talking about in <u>his</u> supreme order and he made the right decision. Had Joe been more careful during the negotiations, he would not be talking like that today.

Before the plebiscite, people like Joe said that America is the best. They had faith in Ambassador Williams and all other U.S. officials in Washington. Now they are saying that the same Americans are liars and are insane. (What a laugh!)

The delay of the Marianas separate administration is not such a bad "blow." Wait until the people find out that they are not going to have their own representative in Washington. They are going to be represented by Honorable Antonio B. Won Pat of Guam. That means that the political status of the Northern Marianas would be equivalent to that of a village on Guam, such as Inarajan or Dededo; ha! So much for thinking that we are going to be better off than Guam.

The Northern Marianas MAY, at its <u>own expense</u>, send a lobbyist to Washington. But that would be a waste of time and money. It would be like sending Honorable Jose R. Cruz out to sea, bare handed, to catch 50 whales. When that is done, let us pray to the Lord.

38 CONGRESS OF MICRONESIA ELECTIONS

November 7, 1975

On December 2, 1975, the Mariana Islands District will hold an election to fill in the vacancy in the lower House of the Congress of Micronesia. For a while I thought that no person from the Marianas would run in this coming election. I thought that no person in the Marianas still has an interest in joining the other Micronesians. Obviously I was wrong. It is pleasing to see that we now have three official candidates running.

A person who expresses a desire to be separated from the rest of Micronesia politically or otherwise, would be a hypocrite to simultaneously express a desire to join the Congress of Micronesia and become united with the other Micronesians. Logically one can only do one or the other.

A parallel situation existed in the Micronesian Constitutional Convention. Those Marianas delegates who opposed unity between the Marianas and the rest of Micronesia either resigned from the convention or did not participate: their actions were consistent with their thoughts. Likewise, those delegates in favor of Micronesian unity satisfactorily participated in the convention. Their actions were also consistent with their thoughts.

Participation in the Congress of Micronesia is of the same nature, except for one thing. When the Marianas becomes a Commonwealth of the Great United States of America, the Marianas Delegation to the Congress of Micronesia will no longer be members of that body but will become members of the District legislature. For them it will be a considerable advancement. Nevertheless, with the advent of the Marianas voting population, one would speculate that no one from the Marianas would want to join the Congress of Micronesia at this point. Instead, they would want to resign. The fact that there are persons from the Marianas who want to join the Congress of Micronesia raises an important question. What do the people of the Marianas truly desire in their relationship with the rest of Micronesia? Obviously they do not know. If they did, the question would not arise.

Asta i otro simana.

39 PLEBISCITE

January 2, 1976
It has been a while since I wrote about the Covenant and the Commonwealth. Recently, a number of people have asked me what is happening to the Covenant. Why is the U.S. Senate taking extra time to approve it? Why is the Marianas not being separated from the other districts? Why are we not receiving all the money we were promised before the plebiscite?

These are very appropriate questions for our citizens to ask. They are entitled to honest answers.

We all know that before the plebiscite our people were bombarded with great promises which the Covenant would bring to them in the very near future. We were promised that the U.S. Congress would anxiously approve the Covenant no later than July of 1975. We were promised that the Marianas would be separated from the other five districts no later than August of 1975. We were promised 1.5 million dollars to finance this separation and the Constitutional Convention. We were promised that the $19,000,000.00 would be appropriated as lease compensation for the Marianas government right away. These are just a few of the many promises made to our people. In response, our people naturally and in good faith went and voted in favor of the Covenant.

Now, where are those promises and why haven't we seen them? Where is Ambassador Williams and his group who made the promises and why haven't we heard from them since we gave them our votes? Where is the 1.5 million dollars and the $19,000,000.00? Where are the fathers of the Covenant from the Marianas and what are they doing? Why don't they talk to us now as they did before the plebiscite?

Some of our leaders declared that if the Covenant were not approved by September of 1975, they would move for independence. It is now 1976. Where is that movement?

The year 1975 brought to our people great lessons about the difficulties in creating a new nation and the value of honesty, sincerity, and quality in leadership. We must have learned from our negotiations with Uncle Sam. Our leaders have learned to work together in the Micronesian Constitutional Convention. We enhanced unity throughout Micronesia by virtue of that Convention.

Should the Covenant not be approved by the U.S. Senate, I will be ashamed to go back to the other districts and say, "I am sorry. I tried to separate from you because I didn't think you were good enough to be associated with me, but I learned two things about myself. First, Uncle Sam doesn't think I am good enough to be associated with him, and second, I cannot stand alone. Therefore, may I please return to you?"

There are great lessons to be learned from our immediate past. Let us look to the future with clearer visions. In 1976, let us properly use the skills and understanding we acquired in 1975.

HAPPY NEW YEAR

40 UNNESESSARY GOVERNMENT TRAVEL

February 20, 1976
Many of our people are now very excited in view of the expected approval of the covenant by the U.S. Senate. Some people give me the impression that they think Christ is about to descend upon them. One cannot realistically predict what the covenant will bring to our people. But we can be certain that some of us will become very successful while others will get skinned alive. We can even predict who are the ones that will greatly benefit and we can conclude that it will be a small minority.

Members of our district legislature appear to be most excited about the approval of the covenant. That we can understand. However, the district legislature does something that I do not understand; that I think is ridiculous; and is harmful to the public. That is, the sending of so many members to Washington, D.C., when there is a congressional hearing on the covenant.

Sending people to Washington is very expensive. The airfare itself cost over one-thousand dollars per person. The per diem paid is very high while the members are receiving their regular salary at the same time. In addition, there is no need to send more than one member to represent the district legislature in the U.S. Congress. Sending five to ten members instead of one will not influence the U.S. Congress. I have stayed in Washington three years and I am aware that congress is more impressed by the appearance of one person who says proper things and in a proper way than fifteen persons who do not say much. I am also aware that when ten of our leaders are sent to Washington, normally only one or two ever speak.

In the interest of the public, the district legislature should not waste the people's money by sending more than one lobbyist to Washington, notwithstanding their excitement about the approval of the covenant.

41 U.S. SENATE APPROVES COVENANT

February 27, 1976
This is a time to rejoice and a time to celebrate. It is a time to laugh and a time to cry.

Congratulations to the people of the Marianas for acquiring what they were made to believe they wanted and congratulations to the United States of America for successfully acquiring a new territory; a small territory which will support and strengthen its military power and influence in the Pacific World and the Far East.

For the people of the Marianas, let us extend a warm congratulations for the many things which they can now be proud of. They can be proud that two-thirds of Tinian, part of Saipan and the whole island north of Saipan now belong to the U.S. military. These lands will be reserved for contingent U.S. military installations and activities. Lord, pray for us.

The people of the Marianas can be proud that they have become a minority out of 220,000,000 people rather than a minority out of 100,000 people. Similarly, they can be proud for becoming second class citizens under a strange flag rather than noble citizens under their previous native flag. I am sure that they cherish more the concept of being inferior to the "mainlanders" than superior to the "district people." It is common knowledge that the people of the

Marianas believe themselves to be superior to the people from other districts of Micronesia and inferior to Americans.

Furthermore, the people of the Marianas can be proud that they are now not represented in their national legislature (U.S. Congress) as they were in the Congress of Micronesia. Whereas, Saipan was the capital of Micronesia, now it is a military stop-over; way out in the Pacific Ocean and only a handful of people ever get to see their great capital, the District of Columbia.

Whereas, the people of the Marianas had priority to any employment before becoming a commonwealth of the U.S., now they do not. Any qualified U.S. citizen is equally entitled to any job in the Marianas as the citizens thereof. The people of the Marianas can be proud of that. It means that many Marianas citizens will get skinned alive when competing for jobs.

However, the people of the Marianas can obviously see something in the commonwealth status which is worth more than anything else. They can see MONEY ($). Money has to be the most important and powerful thing for them. It is more important than brotherhood or sisterhood or family relationship. It is more important than love or religion. It is MONEY which is breaking up homes and family ties on our small islands. It is greed for MONEY which is turning our people cold and bitter. It is greed for money which has caused our people to forget who they are, what is their identity, and to beg for commonwealth status. That they can be proud of and be congratulated for.

Nevertheless, it is money which our people have been praying for, and it is money which they are about to receive. Thanks to Uncle Sam. It is money which he has plenty of, and it is money with which he has purchased us.

CONGRATULATIONS!!!!!!

42 LESSONS FROM AN ESKIMO JURY TRIAL

August 18, 1976
While I was in Washington, D.C., I had an opportunity to describe to a friend the ceremony in which former Ambassador Williams presented the signed Covenant and the United States flag to the people of the Marianas. I explained how our people had tears in their eyes when the ambassador softly added that, "this flag was flown over the U.S. capitol building on the day that the president signed the covenant." While I was telling the story I even had a lump in my throat.

My friend looked at me and with a big surprise on his face he asked, "What is so sentimental about that?" He added, "U.S. flags are flown for a couple of minutes on the Capitol Building and then taken down and given away to tourists." Naturally, that makes such flags really cheap. Of course, I do not know that our new flag from the ambassador was flown only a couple of minutes. However, it is interesting to note that to many Americans, a U.S. flag does not gain significance simply because it is flown over the U.S. Capitol Building.

****

Last week I was in the state of Alaska where I received training from judges and attorneys in court. We worked in the city of Anchorage where most of the people are not Eskimoes. The Eskimoes are living in villages. In one Eskimo village I observed a jury trial where an Eskimo was being tried for manslaughter.

The government's attorney and defense attorney are both law school graduates from Minnesota, and the judge from Michigan. Each of them earns over $40,000.00 annually. Except for the chief of police, who was also Caucasian, the rest of the people are Eskimoes. It appeared that the Eskimo people are mostly uneducated, poor, and did not speak or understand English well.

As I sat there watching the trial, I began to feel as if I were in Micronesia watching a high court trial. I could see the well paid American judges and attorneys running the whole show and imposing upon the Micronesians a system of law that is foreign to them. This is not to say that the situation is bad. In fact, many people think that it is good. Nevertheless, as I sat there, I felt pain in my heart.

It is disappointing that the Micronesians are victims of a drastic imposition of political, economic, and social transformation which result in the people being confused, intimidated, and discouraged. On the other hand, these changes are inevitable. Therefore, the Micronesians should not be intimidated or discouraged. There is no question that we CAN produce our own judges, doctors, engineers, and other professionals. But in order to do that we have to have pride, we have to sweat, and we cannot give up every time we encounter pressure.

We find it easy to blame our shortcomings on the Americans administration. But the easy way out is often the least productive way. It is time to focus our attention not only on where Uncle Sam has failed us, but also on where we have failed ourselves. Obviously we have been sleeping too long. Until we wake up and start to face reality and start being responsible and hardworking, as the American judges and administrators are, we will never be entitled to be our own judges and administrators. We will never be able to earn independence or self-government.

I am hurt that we are being pushed around. At the same time, I realize that we are being provided the opportunity to develop ourselves. If we reject that opportunity, then it will be our own fault when we continue being guarded and governed by outsiders.

43 FEDERAL INCOME TAX

February 5, 1979
When the Covenant was being negotiated between our leaders and the United States, I was then a law student. At that time I was dissatisfied with the Covenant and was opposed to it for many reasons. One of the main reasons why I was opposed to the Covenant was the requirement that the federal income tax be implemented in the Commonwealth. I wrote to the editor then expressing that objection.

The people of the Northern Mariana Islands knew that the federal income tax would be implemented under the Covenant. They were told by the "friends of the Commonwealth" and the promoters of the Covenant that the federal income tax system was good and it was not going to present any problem. As a result, seventy-eight percent (78%) of our people voted in favor of the Covenant and in favor of implementing the federal income tax in the Commonwealth.

Obviously, the people wanted the federal income tax system. They asked for it, and they got it. Now, I do not understand why they do not want to have it. If I was one of those who voted YES for the Covenant, I will not now open my mouth to complain about it. To do so would be like going to a restaurant and ordering spam. Then when the spam is brought out and placed on my table, I would complain that I do not like spam and I do all I could to cancel it and order something else.

I write this letter for an important reason. First, we must learn not to order that which we do not want. Second, before we order, we must first know what we are ordering. Otherwise, if you order federal income tax, you will get federal income tax, and you will eat federal income tax.

44 CONCON CANDIDATES

September 1, 1976

Can a whole day pass without you hearing the word "ConCon," which is short for Constitutional Convention? Of course not. Who will draft our constitution? Who will be our "Founding Fathers?" What kind of constitution should we have? These are our major current concerns which are not easy to resolve.

The candidates have been nominated and the campaigns have been triggered. We now have candidates shouting at the top of their voices, "I am the most qualified to draft a constitution, so and so is not qualified; that party has no qualified candidates; this party has all the qualified candidates" and so forth.

Needless to say, those campaigners who spill such garbage talks are the ones who have no knowledge about constitution. Those who have knowledge about constitution should and will talk about constitution. This is the time and the occasion to talk about what is a constitution and what kind of a constitution will best serve and protect the people of our new commonwealth. This is not the time to publicly discuss who beats up his wife or who does not pay his debts. Such an immature campaign method will only help voters decide who is <u>not</u> qualified, but will not help them decide who <u>is</u>.

The ConCon is very important because the constitution is the most important source of governmental powers and limitations. The constitution will provide how we will form and operate our government. It will be the most powerful and important document setting forth who may be our governor, what will be his obligations, what powers will he have, and how to prevent him from abusing such powers. It will set forth who will make our laws (legislature), what kind of powers will they possess and how to prevent them from abusing such powers against the people. It will also set forth who will interpret and apply our laws (court system), how will they interpret and apply such laws, and how to prevent them from abusing their power to interpret and apply the laws and the constitution itself. The constitution that we will draft must provide for the protection of our fundamental human rights, such as, the right to non-defamatory speech, the right to vote, the right to due process and equal protection of the law, freedom of religion, the right to privacy, the right to liberty and the pursuit of happiness, and many other fundamental rights. It must also provide for the prevention of animalistic treatment of human beings such as slavery, police brutality, cruel and unusual punishment, and unreasonable discrimination based on sex, color, race, religion, or national origin.

These are the subjects that our candidates should be discussing in public. The Constitutional Convention is where our chosen intellectuals and serious minded citizens will meet to draft our destiny and the manner in which we will endeavor to accomplish such destiny. It is not only a political matter, but it is also a judicial, economic, and social matter. Let us be conscientious; let us be serious; and let us choose our "Fore Founding Fathers," not on the basis of vocal quality, but on the basis of intellectual quality and sincerity.

45 A JOKE AND A DREAM

September 15, 1976

One of the major questions that will be considered in the Constitutional Convention is the type of legislative body we will have and the number of members there will be. It has to be determined whether there will be a bicameral or a unilateral legislature. It would also have to be determined how many representative districts there will be and whether the legislators will work on a full-time or a part-time basis.

The Covenant to establish the Commonwealth of the Northern Mariana Islands provides that the Marianas will have a bicameral legislature. I am not sure why such a provision is included in the Covenant, but I believe it is a very impractical and unnecessary provision. A bicameral legislature consisting of more than twenty members, all together including both houses of a full-time basis is unnecessary and excessive. We must not forget that there are less than fifteen thousand people in the Commonwealth of the Northern Mariana Islands. Many of us are tempted to believe that our small islands and population constitute a great nation and a powerful country or a state of a country, but that is not the reality. We are a very small society and we do not need more than fifteen legislators in our legislative branch of the government. In fact, we don't even need full-time legislatures in order to legislate for only less than fifteen thousand people. In comparison, for instance, New York City has approximately seven million people in the city alone, yet it is run merely by a Mayor and a City Council.

Here on our little island, where we have less than fifteen thousand people we are going to have a governor, a lieutenant governor, an attorney general, many departments, a bicameral legislature consisting of the House of Representatives with full-time members all paid at least eight thousand a year ($8,000); a federal district court and a separate court system of the Commonwealth. When you compare the number of people and the kind of problems we have on this island with the kind of government structure that we are dreaming of, it becomes merely a joke and merely a dream.

46 GET OUT

November 5, 1976

A meeting of the Marianas Constitutional Convention was officially set for Friday, October 29, 1976, at 2 in the afternoon. At about that time the delegates took their seats along with the legal consultants; the recording secretary; the radio and newspaper representatives; and other people who came to observe. At 2 p.m. the president of the convention announced that there would be an "executive meeting," and ordered every person to leave the convention hall except the delegates. Persons who were thrown out included the legal consultants; the recording secretary; the media representatives; all other staff of the convention; and the general public. The manner in which people were thrown out was by having the chairman of one substantive committee walk around the room shouting, "OUT! OUT! EVERY ONE NOT A DELEGATE, GET OUT!"

What kind of a constitutional convention are we conducting? I was embarrassed by the manner in which our convention leaders conducted themselves. There is nothing seriously wrong with the convention holding secretive meetings if such meetings are justified. However, such secretive meetings should not be held at a time set for a regular convention hearing which will result in an impolite and embarrassing manner of chasing out people from the convention hall. The secretive meeting could have been set for 4 p.m. when only delegates would be informed and invited.

In addition, the matters discussed during the closed meeting were not secret subjects. They were perfect subjects to be discussed during the regular meetings. Besides, they were not the kind of matters that could be hidden from the public.

In my opinion the convention has no business holding secret meetings. The public has the right to know every bit of action the convention takes. Where the president of the convention picked up the idea of a secretive "EXECUTIVE MEETING" of all the delegates remains a mystery to me. Even our legal consultants from Washington, D.C. appeared shocked.

When this matter was subsequently brought to the attention of the president in the convention, the president responded that the president had the right to call an executive meeting. Okay, the president may have that right, but that is not the point. The point is whether to have a secret meeting and how it should be planned and conducted. It seems so difficult for the president to understand such a simple point.

I hope it will not happen again.

47 CONCON POLITICS

November 12, 1976

The constitutional convention of the Northern Mariana Islands has met for 20 days as of Nov. 10th. It is supposed to have met for 25 consecutive days, but the convention did not meet for 5 days as the law which established the convention and required that it meet for <u>50 consecutive</u> days.

There is a great deal about the convention and its leadership and committee activities which I would like to write about, but time and space will not permit. However, the people of the Northern Marianas are entitled to know what is happening in the convention and I will devote my next few columns to this subject.

On the first day of the convention, October 18, 1976, it became clear that the leadership of this convention will not be selected on the basis of personal qualification and experience, but on the basis of political affiliation. Despite all the sentimental and heart-breaking speeches by the president and delegates calling for the members to forget their social and political differences and to commit their fullest effort to the success of this historic event, the majority party (territorial party) clearly manipulated the activities of the first day to make sure that only members of their party will hold the office of the president, the three vice-presidents, the floor leader, the secretary and the committee chairmanship and vice-chairmanship. By changing the proposed rules of procedure the president was empowered to appoint members of his majority party to certain positions and the same party is empowered to control the activities of the convention by a vote of a simple majority.

The office of the floor leader is a creation of the majority party without any justification or need. A floor leader is needed when the president is incapable or assumed to be lacking in his ability to conduct the meeting of the convention.

Within a few days of the convention it became evident that the real conflict within the convention is not between the political parties, but between Rota, Tinian, and Saipan delegations. The conflict between these delegations is so important and so complicated that I will devote a whole column to such subject.

For the moment let us simply ask whether the leadership of this convention will be effective and productive. It will demonstrate whether leadership which is acquired not by way of democratic election but by way of political manipulation and appointment is functional and effective.

On the first day of the convention there was a meeting between a few members of the majority and minority parties. The legal consultants were also present. During the course of that meeting, the president of the convention was expressing his views when one of his party members ordered him to <u>shut up</u> and to let only the other members talk on behalf of their party. Such a gesture toward the president is an insult to that office; especially when it is coming from their own group. It clearly illustrates the lack of respect for and confidence in our leadership.

At the end of this convention we will be able to assess better the product of our political-minded delegations. If the convention continues to function the way it has been, we will not have a constitution at the end of this convention.

48 GENERALLY GOOD

February 24, 1977

"I came back and I am glad I did." This column has been absent since the beginning of the Constitutional Convention. The convention took so much of my time that I was not able to continue writing in this column. After the constitutional convention, I returned to my law office and found such a pile of work that I could not resume writing. In January of this year I started teaching an extension course from the University of Guam and that added to the work load involved. As a result, I even had to resign from the committee on public education for the constitution. Now that things are back to normal and I have some time to write, I hope that I will be able to writ this column every week.

Speaking of the constitution, which is the major matter of concern at this time, we must not forget that we ought to go out and vote yes or no in the referendum set for March 6, 1977. The constitution which has been signed by the majority of the delegates to the convention is a generally good constitution. It is a constitution that will establish a government of the people, by the people, and for the people. It will form a government that is guaranteed to function and it will be a government that will not overburden the taxpayers for its operation expenses. However, I am using the term generally good because there are aspects of the constitution which are not very favorable and which is not very democratic.

In particular, I am referring to that part of the constitution which provides that the senate will have the power of confirmation of all department heads, judges, and other officials which are to be appointed by the governor. We must realize that the senate which consists of nine senators; three from Saipan, three from Tinian and three from Rota is a body of lawmakers which is controlled by the minority communities on Tinian and Rota. Rota and Tinian have a population together of not more than 2,500. On the other hand, Saipan has a population of approximately 13,000 people. However, in looking at the composition of the senate it appears that the 2,500 people are represented by six senators while the 13,000 are represented by three senators. This is such an unequal and unfair representation that it is directly contrary or against the principle of democracy. Since the minorities in Rota and Tinian have such a great power in the senate and since the senate is the body that confirms appointments of the governor, it is very easy for the minorities in Rota and Tinian to control the person who is appointed by the governor and therefore the department which is headed by that person. If this person who has been confirmed by the senate refuses to comply with the desires of the minorities in Rota and Tinian, he can be assured that the next time around he will not be confirmed by the senate. This is a power that is so great, a power that is supposed to be possessed only by a majority in a democratic society, but which has been given to a very small minority in the Northern Marianas.

The most basic principle of democracy is that the majority of the people govern and that the minority of people follow the desires of the majority. What our constitution has done with respect to the power of confirmation is that it has given the power to govern to the minority and has required the majority to comply with the desires of the minority. This is also contrary to the democratic principle of one man, one vote policy.

On the surface, it appears that this section of our constitution is contrary to the constitution of the United States. However, the lawyers for the constitutional convention are of the opinion that because the geographic and demographic setting of our community and our commonwealth is so different from the United States, that we are entitled to a different consideration and standard of measurement. They think that our constitution will stand up on the U.S. Supreme Court, but, of course, they cannot guarantee that.

It is my personal feeling that because this provision of the constitution is undemocratic and there is a likelihood that this provision will be abused by the minority in an effort to gain power and influence in government, that the majority of the people of the Northern Marianas will soon make an amendment to this constitution to change this portion of the constitution. During the constitutional convention, there was a tremendous movement by certain members of the Saipan delegation to change this part of the constitution and not to give so much power to the minority. However, it was very difficult to do so, because the law which established the constitutional convention provided that if the municipality of Rota or Tinian is not represented in the convention, that the convention cannot proceed or cannot act until such municipality is represented. During the course of the debates, it was made very clear by the delegates from Rota and Tinian that if this power of confirmation was not given to the minority, that the minority would boycott the constitutional convention and that would have prevented or stopped the constitutional convention from proceeding and it would have prevented the drafting of any constitution. It was a law which was obviously not done very carefully, and, as a result, it will require more work, money and time, because it will be necessary to amend the constitution in the near future.

In closing, however, I must agree that the constitution is generally a good constitution and I hope that it will be approved by the people of the Northern Marianas. The constitution is now not perfect, but it can be improved just like the U.S. Constitution has been greatly improved by the 26 amendments that have been made to it.

49 MARIJUANA LEGISLATION

August 2, 1974

Permit me to congratulate Ben Abrams, the people's defender, for his success in the marijuana case. Permit me also to discredit his integrity for his statements with regard to marijuana and the Trust Territory.

As quoted in the Marianas Variety, July 26, 1974, Abrams said, "It is hoped that Congress will use restraint in introducing any new laws concerning the prohibition of marijuana, because the present legal status allows for an excellent opportunity to study any social effects cause by its legalization." Our good defender wants to use us, Micronesians, as a "STUDY". Americans would probably say that he wants to use us as "GUINEA PIGS". Gentle Ben does not realize that there are 120,000 of us and there is only one of him. I hope he thinks twice before he starts on his experimentation.

Our good defender also said something to the effect that Micronesia is now the most enlightened and sophisticated place in the world because marijuana is legalized. In other words, by allowing our people to smoke marijuana, we become enlightened and sophisticated. This is the most offensive and misleading statement we Micronesians have encountered lately.

The judge did not legalize marijuana because it is good or because he thinks it is not harmful, he made his decision loosely on the grounds that the present law is not good because it gives too much authority to the director of Health Services and provides for a penalty that is unreasonable in comparison with the opium and heroin prohibition laws.

The Congress should make a new law prohibiting the use of marijuana but it should not permit that Micronesians be used as a "STUDY" on the effects of marijuana.

50 THE OPPOSITE OF SMART

March 7, 1975
The Municipal Council of Tinian is very smart in prohibiting slot machines on their island. Even most states in the U.S. are smart in preventing slot machines from destroying their good citizens. Guam is smart in prohibiting slot machines. Our District Administrator is smart in vetoing the gambling bill enacted by our district legislature. This veto protects our people.

However, those members of our district legislature who are pushing to legalize gambling on Saipan are not smart. They are the opposite of being smart. They are more interested in filling their own pockets than in protecting the goodwill of our citizens.

51 FREEDOM OF THE PRESS

August 1, 1975

It is disheartening to learn that certain leaders in our developing community are trying to suppress our small newspapers and discourage the free flow of news and communication. Suppression of the news media is a sure way to breed secrecy and corruption in the government. There is hardly any justification for our small government to hide its activities and plans from the public.

In our elective democratic form of government, where the people are supposed to dictate what the government should do in the interest of the people, there is an absolute necessity for a continuous free flow of news and communication between the government institutions and the people and also among the people themselves.

Any economic, political and social developments on our islands would necessitate greater development of our news media. Our people would be served and protected more if we support our newspapers and the disclosure of our public activities and public concerns than if we suppress them. It is for these reasons that freedom of the press is guaranteed under the Constitution of the United States. This freedom does not only guarantee the disclosure of news information but also the expression of personal opinions by individuals as well as the newspapers.

We must not forget that <u>Washington Post</u> and other newspapers played a major role in the prosecution of the "Watergate Scandal" in Washington D.C. and the restoration of freedom to the American people.

52 POLICE BRUTALITY

October 10, 1975
Did you know that there is such a thing as police brutality on this friendly little island? Police brutality is where an uneducated and untrained police officer uses brutal force to coerce our citizens to incriminate themselves. This happens when a police officer thinks that he is the law or that he is above the law.

This is a terrible mistake. It is a disgrace that we do not need on this island. If our police officers are well educated and well trained, and our police department is efficient, they would not have to resort to kicking our citizens, punching our citizens, and beating up our citizens in order to accomplish their objective. Their objective being to make this a safe, peaceful and enjoyable island.

When a person is arrested for any crime, the arresting police officer has the duty under the law to explain to the arrested person the following:

1. That he has the right to remain silent so that he would not incriminate himself.
2. That everything he voluntarily says may be used against him.
3. That he has a right to have a lawyer and that the police will help in getting a lawyer at that moment, not the following day or thereafter.

Some of our police officers do not follow their duties. Instead, they beat up our citizens in order to coerce them to make statements against themselves. Little do they know that coerced confession is not admissible as evidence in court.

If this disgraceful practice does not cease now, our full-time district legislature must do something.

Asta i otro simana.

53 ROTA FIESTA

October 17, 1975
The fiesta on Rota last weekend was a great success. It was also a great lesson. The people on Rota still maintain the warm community spirit which does two things. First, it makes their little community peaceful and pleasant, and second, it gives the community the courage, the facility, and the ability to accommodate and serve all the hundreds of visitors who come to celebrate the day of their patron Saint every year.

The excitement started with the arrival of so many new faces; some with big smiles as they reunite with relatives or old friends, and some with no smiles for they were not sure where to stay or how to get to the village. Next came the slaughtering of the pigs and other activities in preparation for the party. It seemed that many visitors had never seen pigs slaughtered. They watched with interest, took pictures, and asked questions.

Then came the big day: Sunday, October 12. The elaborate mass service started at 10:00 a.m. with Bishop Flores saying the mass. Following what was the indescribably fantastic food service. Those who were punctual were lucky to try the fruit bats, coconut crabs and deer meat. Those bats were so good that some people took whole ones for themselves. While people were eating, drinking, socializing, etc., the Micronesian traditional dancers from Saipan came and took over the show. They were good and the people enjoyed their performance very much.

They say that every year the number of visitors to the Rota fiesta doubles that of the previous year. I can understand why. I would recommend that people go and witness for themselves the beauty and power of culture, tradition, and community spirit.

Asta i otro semana.

54 MICRONESIANIZATION

October 24, 1975
Today there is a great deal of emphasis on Micronesianization. That is, placing Micronesians and replacing expatriates in key positions and other government positions. This is a good practice and is likely to be continued. It is a practical way of training our citizens and promoting self-government.

In the Marianas, however, there is a practice that is contrary to the principle of Micronesianization. That is the practice of bringing in so many non-resident workers in the private business sector. Our construction companies in particular and other enterprises hire more outsiders than Micronesians. Certainly they have reasons for doing so. Primarily there are positions that cannot be filled by qualified Micronesians. In addition, there may not be enough Micronesian laborers and finally, the available Micronesians may not want to work or are too expensive.

Of course, we do not have ill feelings against outsiders. Most of them on our islands are peaceful, respectable, and productive people. They contribute substantially to our economic development.

However, it is evident that the importation of labor is contrary to the development of our people. It is already a common expression that the Chamorros are spoiled and lazy. They will not do construction work. They will not farm and they will not fish. By bringing in outside workers to do this work, the Chamorros become more spoiled and will eventually be totally deprived of these skills. For instance, we are witnessing that most entertainers on Saipan are outsiders. This situation kills the incentive among our young people to start out as amateurs and eventually become professional entertainers. When our people find out that the outsiders are much more skilled and are no match for them, they become discouraged from competition.

As an attorney, I have encountered too many domestic problems created by non-resident workers. In about forty percent of our divorce cases and other domestic relations cases, a non-resident worker is seriously involved. In addition, the non-resident workers create immigration problems and contract problems. There is evidence that many of them transfer illegally from one employer to another employer causing fights between two or more employers.

If our Administration and Legislatures do not act to control this problem our islands will eventually and be greatly controlled by outsiders. It is not their fault and we do not dislike them. We simply should not allow ourselves and our community to be run over as a result of our careless, laziness and lack of leadership.

Asta i otro simana.

55 FAIR AND EQUAL TREATMENT

November 21, 1975
We all know that as the number of foreigners in Micronesia increases there will be more interaction and conflict between Micronesian and non-Micronesian. This is natural. It should be expected and should be understood by both the Micronesian and the foreigner. There is, however, a general attitude among Micronesians which is also natural and should be expected, but which is discriminatory, unconstitutional, unorthodox, and should be discouraged. Such attitude being that if a conflict arises between a Micronesian government, any other institution or by any Micronesian person. Furthermore, the general feeling being that in case of such conflict, only the Micronesian should receive help from any other Micronesian.

For example, Micronesian Legal Services Corporation have often been criticized for representing "outsiders" against Micronesians in domestic relations, employment contracts and other legal problems. The Public Defender's Office has been criticized for representing "outsiders" who have been accused of a crime against a Micronesian. I (a Micronesia) have personally been criticized for extending legal help to Korean fishermen who were accused of illegal fishing in Micronesian waters. Carlos Salii was criticized for representing the Continental Hotel against the people of Saipan.

No doubt, it would be to the benefit of certain Micronesians if no help or protection is given to their competitive foreign rivals. It may even be in the interest of Micronesia not to give legal protection to Korean or Japanese fishermen so that their valuable ships and fishing equipments be expropriated and used by the government.

Nevertheless, despite all these Micronesian interests, there are other factors which are more fundamental, more important and should be given greater respect.

To invidiously discriminate against foreign nationals solely on the basis of their being foreigners is an unfair and abominable policy and practice. When a Micronesian travels to or sojourns in any foreign country we anticipate and appreciate he is being treated equally with citizens of that country. We expect that he be protected by its laws. Otherwise, if he is treated less than humanely, we would become insulated and humiliated. For that reason, we would become insulted and humiliated. For that reason, we too must treat foreigners in our country equally with our citizens and give them the same legal protection.

I am not suggesting that any and all foreigners be admitted unfettered into Micronesia. Nor that they should not be classified or discriminated within reasonable bounds. The number and the nature of immigrants admitted into Micronesia ought to be regulated. Yet once admitted, they become practically part of the Micronesians and should be treated accordingly. They are not to be treated as though they are less than human.

The idea that a Micronesian should favor only Micronesian is a primitive concept. It is a concept that was practicable in the days when Micronesia did not communicate with or depend on the rest of the world. Today Micronesia is inevitably an integral part of the world's communication, commercial, and cultural network. We can no longer remain selfish or isolated. We must face the realities of the modern world and perpetuate our growth like a responsible nation.

56 THAT DOES NOT MAKE SENSE

November 28, 1975
I drove by the new airport at Isley Field the other day and I was quite impressed. The terminal building is not finished but it is huge and very artistic. I am certainly very proud of it and can hardly wait until it is opened in December of this year. Unfortunately our new airport lacks a control tower or a flight service station which is very essential to have at an airport. Even our present small airport has a flight service station.

I understand that the present flight service station at Kobler Field will continue to provide the same services when the new airport is opened at Isley Field. But that does not make sense. How can you have the airport at Isley and the radio room at Kobler. The radio man will not be able to see either the airport or the airplane. How can the radio man effectively guide the airplanes when landing or taking off from the airport? Perhaps the F.A.A. or the Airport Authority will be able to explain.

In another matter I would like to enlighten our people about a rumor which is of great importance. The rumor pertains to Dr. Benusto Kaipat, whom I am not acquainted with as a person or as a medical doctor. However, it is only fair that Dr. Kaipat be made aware that many people on Saipan have negative attitudes towards the way he relates to his patients and the proficiency of his medical treatments.

I do not know anything about Dr. Kaipat's personality or as a doctor and I cannot evaluate him. But I have heard too many rumors that his patients are dissatisfied.

To remedy this, the patients should not spread rumors among the people. They should relate it to the doctor so that he could do something about it.

57 TRAFFIC PROBLEMS

December 12, 1975

The people of the Marianas are proud that the roads in their district are the best in Micronesia, thanks to the U.S. military. After building the old Isley Field, the military had a huge amount of extra asphalt and decided to make use of it by building a highway around Saipan. Our roads are generally good, but there is much to be desired.

The bumps in the villages should have been painted a year or so ago when they were put up. We need more traffic signs indicating bumps, curves, hills, intersections, speed limits, etc. Many of the signs that we do have are facing the wrong directions or placed too close or too far from the intended viewer. In the days when Saipan had few visitors, traffic signs were not so important for two reasons.

First, there was little traffic and second, most drivers were Saipanese who knew the roads well. Today we have lots of the traffic and outsiders. With the opening of the big airport there will be even more visitors and more traffic. Therefore, without adequate traffic directions our roads will become unsafe.

It is good that a new highway is built between the new airport and San Vicente. But San Vicente has less than 20% of our population. The new highway should have been built between the airport and Chalan Kanoa where about 50% of the people live.

I am speculating that our government is going to make the same stupid mistake that Guam made in delaying the improvement of roads. Beach Road between Chalan Kanoa and San Jose is due for traffic lights. But our government will wait until the people are getting killed weekly before it will expand the road and put up lights.

Texas Road is due to be repaired and paved in order to reduce traffic on Beach Road, but the government will not do it until the improved Beach Road becomes inadequate.

If our government does not begin to implement plans to prevent traffic problems in the near future, we will be pulling our left ear to touch the right ear.

58 AIRPORT WOES

January 23, 1976
There is another great lesson that we ought to learn from the incredible problems we now face with respect to our beautiful new airport. I believe we have the biggest, the most modern and the most authentic air terminal in this part of the world including Guam. We have been very proud and we're all looking forward to the grand opening in July. Even the temporary opening celebration was quite elaborate.

Now we are told that there will not be any plane (other than the Continental's small 727 jet) landing on our new airport for at least another year. We built a multi-million dollar airport with a capacity to accommodate 707 and 747 jets. We built our hopes and dreams about the expected "Boom" in tourism. We all expect for Uncle Sam to hand us out millions of dollars under a commonwealth status. We built and beg for money, then we build more and beg for more money. But we don't stop for a moment to consider whether the things we're building or begging for are necessary or whether we're ready for them.

Now what do we have? We have an unfinished airport that is expected to go bankrupt, unless each air passenger is taxed $2.50 every flight. It would not be used to even half its full capacity. Logically, 12,000 people do not need such a huge monster. It's a burden upon our small community especially now that we're not going to have the big "Boom" in tourism and all related businesses. We can't even be sure that we'll have all the millions of dollars under commonwealth to help out.

What should we do? Primarily, we should start thinking and learning. What is the most important thing to do. It is okay to build and to have high hopes, but there is a point where things may get out of hand, become excessive, or impractical. While our people have such a fantastic air terminal to show off, at the same time many of them are embarrassed to take foreign visitors to their homes because their roads are dusty, bumpy, muddy, and their houses are unsanitary or otherwise disgusting.

These are situations that illustrate our readiness to become self-governing. It is these misfortunes that should indicate how capable our government is. Are we really ready? Look around! The next thing you'll see is a football stadium with the capacity to sit 100,000 people; even though there are only 12,000 of us. Yet you won't see the roads expanded and improved until traffic problems get out of hand. Are we ready?

59 RADIO RECOMMENDATIONS

February 13, 1976

I hate to criticize our radio station, KJQR, because it is a good radio and it provides our communities with an indispensable flow of news communication, entertainment and education. But with good intentions I wish to point out that there needs to be some improvement made in one of our radio announcers. I cannot mention any name because I frankly do not know. However, this announcer will benefit himself in his career if he would work harder on his English pronunciation and intonation patter. This is important only for purposes of broadcasting. It does not matter how anybody talks privately. But a radio broadcast should be done with a certain degree of quality and acceptability.

Other persons have expressed similar reactions and I am sure that such an improvement will be appreciated by a large number of people.

I write this with the realization that it takes time and hard work for any person to learn a foreign language and become a good broadcaster in that language. A person should be given time and a chance to progress in his vocation. However, it is also a matter of common sense that after certain time is given, certain improvement is expected.

60 SELF RELIANCE

March 5, 1976

The people of the Marianas have until approximately 1980 to prepare for self-government under the commonwealth status. Obtaining a commonwealth status is one thing. Running a commonwealth government is quite a different thing. I hate to think that when the covenant is implemented in its entirety, after the termination of the Trusteeship Agreement, outsiders may have to be hired to run our government because we are not ready to run it ourselves. Excuse me; I mean fellow Americans might have to come from across the ocean to run our government and business affairs. Isn't this the case now?

However, this does not have to happen. We can and we ought to put major emphasis on educating, training and preparing our own people in every vocation that is relevant on these islands. The problem is, we cannot educate or train people who are basically lazy and have no confidence in themselves. That is where our problem lies. Most of our people will not go to school if the government does not pay their school expenses and a salary. They want to get paid for going to school. What kind of attitude is that?

The government, and especially our government, cannot and will not pay everybody to go to school. For four years while I was in college, the Trust Territory government denied my applications for scholarship. And for two years in law school, the same government denied my applications for scholarship. Had I decided to depend on our government, I would not have gone to college or law school. Instead, I would be floating around these islands also, praying for commonwealth also, so that we may have free school lunches, free USDA food, free welfare benefits, free Medicare, and all the other handouts from great Uncle Sam. The point is, that the people have to want to put in some effort, before any achievement can result.

We have to understand that it is only through sweating and laboring that we can advance ourselves with pride and dignity. We cannot do it by selling our precious lands and begging other countries for handouts here, handouts there, and gambling everywhere.

Until we learn this principle and begin to act and live accordingly, we will never become self-governing.

Amen.

61 DUE PROCESS RIGHTS

March 13, 1976

I have worked as a public defender for six months and I have discovered that approximately ninety-nine percent of our people are unaware of their constitutional rights to due process when arrested by police officers. One of the main reasons why our police officers are able and willing to abuse their authority or trick people into making confessions is that the people themselves do not know what the police can and cannot do according to the law. If the people are aware what the police officers are supposed to do, they will do their jobs correctly. Otherwise, they will be criticized and they will have difficulty prosecuting cases.

When a person is picked up or arrested for suspicion of a crime, the police cannot ask that person about that crime right away. First, the officer has to explain to the arrested person two things.

1. That he has a right to remain silent and anything he says may be used against him.

2. That he has a right to have a lawyer and a lawyer will be called for him or he may call is own lawyer.

The police officer is not allowed to force a person to say anything about the crime. If he does force the person to make a statement, that statement is not valid in court. Therefore, if the person gives a statement because the officer beats him up or threatens to beat him or put him in jail, that statement becomes invalid in court.

Also, if the person says he wants a lawyer, and the officer takes his statement before the lawyer gets there, that statement is also invalid in court. Police officers have the habit of telling the arrested person that there is no lawyer available and that he will have to stay in jail until one is available, unless, he gives a statement. Any statement given under such coercion is also invalid in court.

Most people and most police officers believe that a person may be detained in jail for 24 hours without any reason. That is not true. A person may be detained for not more than twenty four hours, if he has not been charged with a crime but is a suspect, and _only if_ the _person_ is going to be examined. That includes taking blood samples, hair samples, finger prints and the like. But only for those purposes.

If our citizens and the police officers understand the above principles, they will be able to communicate and understand each other. Until that happens, the desire for democracy and due process on our islands will remain a dream.

62 MARIANAS VARIETY FOURTH ANNIVERSARY

March 3, 1976

This issue marks the fourth anniversary of the Marianas Variety News. I wish to congratulate the publisher, the editor, and all the staff of this magnificent paper. It has not been easy for them to keep operating for four years. They have been threatened with lawsuits and have been ridiculed by our "fearless leaders." In fact, a political leader once threatened to destroy this important paper as soon as we become a Commonwealth of the United States.

If the good leader honestly plans to do that and believes he can actually do it, then he is looking for trouble. How then would he communicate his good messages to his good people?

Anybody who thinks that Commonwealth will bring us further freedom and democracy is wise and sensible. But anybody who thinks that Commonwealth means the suppression of news media, the deprivation of our citizens' freedom of speech and of the press, and anybody who thinks that Commonwealth will facilitate and allow secrecy and clandestine activities in our government operation is uninformed, misled, and is likely to get in trouble.

We must not forget the recent Watergate scandal in the District of Columbia. We must not forget that Watergate was the product of secrecy and clandestine activities within the U.S. Federal

Government. We must also not forget that our fellow Americans are not proud of that scandal. And most important, we must not forget that it was the news media which brought the scandal into the open and partially eliminated the disease.

The Marianas Variety has done its share in promoting discussions and open communications about our economic, social and political situation. Through this paper, we have learned the good side and the bad side of the Covenant. We have learned what our legislature has done which it shouldn't and what is hasn't done which it should. I can list endlessly the many things that we learn from this paper. I can even list many good things that people do because of the paper and many bad things which people will not do because of the paper.

A newspaper is very important in an intellectual and democratic society, such as many of us think we have. It is very important for the people to know what the leaders and government are thinking and doing. It is also very important for the leaders and the government to know what the people are thinking and doing. Without such understanding, we cannot have a government of the people, by the people and for the people. But most important, if we do not have a newspaper, we cannot have such an understanding between our people and the government.

The Marianas Variety obviously facilitates and promotes that understanding. We ought to be thankful. We also ought to support and congratulate our newspapers.

CONGRATULATIONS!!

63 SCRUBBING OUR OWN FLOORS

May 4, 1976
I went alone to a local night club last night after working late hours and I made a very interesting observation. Let me share it with you.

I walked quietly in and sat myself at an empty table facing the band. I ordered a drink and started to relax, enjoying the music and watching people dance. Different waitresses would chat with me for a minute or two. Then as I looked around I began to realize something interesting. The people behind the bar counter were all foreigners. The five waitresses were all foreigners. The four men and the lady singer in the band were foreigners. The people on the dance floor were all foreigners. The people at the other tables were all foreigners.

There I was; a Saipanese in a Saipan local night club; in a Saipan village; on a regular week night; in the midst of people from other places; feeling like I was in a different country. I could not even speak my own language.

Certainly we do not have negative feelings towards people from other places who work on Saipan. We brought them here in the first place. Also, it is natural and very logical that people will seek better employment under better conditions which offer better income.

Even Saipanese do that. Many Saipanese left for Guam and the U.S. when Saipan was part of the Trust Territory. Now that we are a U.S. Commonwealth, many of them are returning and creating all sorts of legal, political and social problems. That will be the subject of my next week's column.

Let's get back to foreign labor. As we bring in hundreds of foreign laborers to do our work, hundreds of our own people are desperate for jobs. Does that make sense?

Of course business persons and employers feel that it makes sense to bring in cheap laborers who are willing to work and it does not make sense to hire local, expensive workers who are not willing to work. But whose interest are we to give priority to? Are we to give priority to the interests of the few business persons or are we to give priority to the interest of the general public?

I call upon our people and our government to think about this matter seriously. We must get down on our knees and scrub our own floors. We must do that for ourselves today. If we don't do that for ourselves today, we will be forced to do it not only for ourselves but for others in the future.

We must plan now while things are ahead of us. We will not be able to look ahead once things are behind us.

64 WHAT HAPPENED TO GRANDMA'S LAND?

May 11, 1976
Before we voted in favor of becoming a U.S. Commonwealth I used to write letters to the editor predicting things that would happen if we were to become a Commonwealth. One of the things I predicted was that there would be an influx of people from Guam, Hawaii and the Mainland, and other places, looking for jobs and a "better place to live." There is an indication that this is now becoming a reality although it is at a very low scale. No doubt, for many people, Saipan is a better place to live in than many other parts of the world.

We are witnessing an increasing number of Saipanese-Guamanians who left Saipan aeons ago, and are now coming back. Many of these former Saipanese left for Guam looking for better jobs, modern environment, and a better life. Most of them probably found a better life since they stayed for many years, suggesting to their relatives back on Saipan that they were never coming back. Today, Guam is hard hit with employment problems, crimes, and over crowdedness. At the same time, the Northern Marianas seems to be coming ahead very nicely. As a natural result, people want to "go back home to Saipan." That's cool. That's natural, and we don't have anything against it. But here is where the problem arises.

These people had courage and determination so they left Saipan, giving their relatives the impression that they were never coming back. As a result, their relatives did many things which they thought were good for their family without consultation with their relatives who had left for good. Now, the relatives who left years ago, are coming back and raising the following questions:

1. Why did you build your concrete house on that land without my knowledge?
2. Why did you distribute our grandma's land among yourselves without my participation?
3. Why did you sell grandpa's land without my approval?

There are many other questions raised and some are related to other matters. This is also natural and expected to happen, but there's more to it than that. Many of these questions are now turning into court cases. It won't be long before we will be witnessing a series of court actions between families and relatives.

Whether this is good or bad is a matter of personal opinion, and I will not make any suggestion. Nevertheless, we should be aware of this problem, and we should try to settle our family conflicts without having to resort to the courts. I realize that those of us who are affected with this problem are highly disturbed. But we should also realize that these are natural consequences of becoming a U.S. Commonwealth. We should be ready to accept them and deal with them properly.

65 CAN YOU HEAR ME NOW?

May 18, 1976

When we think about it, Saipan is truly an advanced island compared to any other island in the Trust Territory and islands in the South Pacific. We have water shortages during dry seasons, but it is nothing serious. We have adequate electricity; an okay road system; an okay radio system, except for the massacre of the English language; our T.V. system is probably okay; but our telephone system? We appreciate having a telephone system, but we have to do something to improve it.

I don't understand why in the afternoons it is very difficult to call the Capitol Hill area from Chalan Kanoa area. I don't understand why you cannot call certain numbers from certain numbers, you'd have to call the operator and have her call for you. Why is it that a lot of telephones stop working when it rains? Why do you get a busy signal even when the number you are dialing is not busy? Why is it that when you dial a certain number, another number will ring or else two separate numbers will be ringing at the same time? Several times, I have dialed a number and two people answer from two separate phone numbers. It will be fun if you can control which two separate numbers will ring. Then you'll have a trio, but you cannot control it. Finally, why do people pay a set monthly fee for a phone that does not give a set monthly service? I don't understand these things, but I do understand it when a person slams the telephone and cusses at whoever is responsible.

In an advanced and sophisticated American society, such as ours, where we have senators and will soon have a governor and Washington representative; we must have a telephone system that works. We have already had an alleged armed robbery on this island. That is a sign of "progress." However, it will be ridiculous if a man cannot call for help when his wife is raped on a rainy night because his phone does not work when it rains.

We have received good news from our four law students in New Guinea. One of the things they mention is that the telephone system in New Guinea is perfect, compared to here. New Guinea was a Trust Territory for many years, until recently. It was administered by Australia. If Australia could set up such a good telephone system for its Trust Territory, why couldn't the United States?

66 ON WAR CLAIMS

August 25, 1976

Hurray to the War Claims Commission. The commission has done its job and while some people are dissatisfied, many people are happy. A great number of our people have become rich overnight. There are people who never owned a car in their lives, but are now driving a Toyota or Datsun. I have heard of people who never wore a watch before, but are now wearing the most expensive gold watches. There are also people who have fixed their houses or built a new one. All this became possible as a result of the war claims payments. On the other hand, there are those people who wasted most of their new wealth in gambling, drinking, and other destructive manners. We are very lucky that the slot machines were banned from our island before the claim payments were made.

We should be grateful to the governments of the U.S. and Japan. Personally, I don't think that our people have been compensated adequately or fairly, and I think it was a mistake for the U.S. and Japan to have waited this long to make their compensation. Nevertheless, many people are satisfied because they have been able to improve their lifestyle.

The biggest problems with the war claims are not visible at this time. But there are tremendous conflicts that have occurred among family members and other relatives. Some of the biggest and most complex lawsuits filed recently have to do with war claim money distribution. In many instances, a claim is filed by one person on behalf of all the heirs of his ancestor. The money is then paid to that single claimant with the understanding that he will distribute it equally among all the heirs. Unsurprisingly, many such individual trustees decided to keep all the money to themselves, depriving the relatives of their shares. Then there are those people who feel that children of their dead brothers or sisters are not entitled to war claim money. There are many other types of related problems and many of them will end in court.

There is a lesson to be learned from this. Money is like a devil. It is tempting and corrupting. Many people have been blinded by money and have lost their sight of the value and beauty of brotherhood and sisterhood. If they would only learn that money comes and goes. They may have a thousand dollars today, but may not have it next week. But if you hurt your friends and relatives and you ruin your reputation, it is very difficult to redeem yourself.

Those people who have cheated their own blood must reconsider the situation. This is the time to settle such problems. They are not necessary, and they must not wait for the court to make that decision for them.

67 BEAUTIFY CNMI

October 4, 1976

I took the liberty of driving around the beautiful island of Saipan this last weekend, just to relax, to enjoy and to observe the scenery. Generally speaking, I was pleased with the type of roads, the type of houses and the beaches that we have on this quiet little island. However, there is one very important matter that is very disgusting and I wish people will begin to do something about it. That refers to all the trash and garbage that people drop on the side of the roads, on the road itself, and other public places including the beach. In addition, we even see dead dogs, cats, and other dead animals laying on the highways. It is difficult to find an answer to this problem, but it is a detrimental problem and our government has to innovate some type of project to alleviate this problem. The situation is certainly very unhealthy, unsanitary and ugly. It demonstrates the degree of illiteracy and characterizes many of our citizens. It demonstrates the lack of realization and appreciation for cleanliness, health, and beauty. Perhaps it is very natural that some of our people are of that nature and that we may not expect them to know or to be any better. Nevertheless, I believe that if we are going to continue to progress, if we are going to become part of the American political family, if we are going to govern ourselves and become responsible citizens, we must enforce a type of law that will guarantee that our island will be kept clean, safe, attractive and able to give our people pride in themselves.

This is the type of problem that can be studied and solved by our legislature and our health department. I do not understand why our legislators have been so oblivious to an obvious and sickening situation on our island, in our villages and even in some homes. Certainly laws can be made and laws can be enforced which will prohibit, prevent and stop any and all dumping of garbage on our roads and in our villages. It is not difficult to make such laws and to enforce them. It also does not take a genius to recognize such problems and to find means to combat the same.

If our government and our people continue to ignore the need for sanitation and control of garbage disposal, we will soon become a pest to the rats, cockroaches, and maggots. We have already been conquered by the African snails and the termites. As a result, we can no longer farm or build wooden houses.

What are we and our government doing about it? We are sitting back, drinking our beers, and thinking that everything is going swell.

68 POWER OUTAGE

October 8, 1976
Recently I have been chatting with several students and teachers from the Marianas High School, and they seem very concerned about a serious problem that they are all facing. Since September 9th, 1976, two days after the school opened, the entire school has been without electricity. It is anticipated that the school will not have electricity for several more weeks or months. It appears that an electrical device that is necessary for the supply of electricity to the school has broken down and needs replacement. However, our government does not have such a device in stock and it needs to be ordered from the States. Needless to say, it might take several months before such an order arrives.

For many of us who are not teachers or students of the school we may not appreciate the difficulties that result from this lack of power. But we should appreciate the extent to which our children are suffering. Naturally certain subject areas will suffer more severely than others, but they all suffer nonetheless.

In the field of vocational education there is a tremendous problem. These subjects are highly dependent upon electric power machines in the teaching of carpentry, mechanics, and other areas. In the area of science, the science laboratory is virtually inoperative without electricity. The same thing is true in homemaking courses. Naturally all the kitchen appliances run by electricity are useless without power. In the area of social studies, there are many filmstrips that are supposed to be shown to the students but cannot be shown because of the lack of electricity. Recently there was a film that had to be shown at the district legislature building across the street from the school campus. It is fortunate that the legislature is kind enough to help out under the circumstances.

There is no doubt that the teachers and students could get very frustrated because they cannot function in the classrooms. The result of all this is a detriment to our educational system, especially at the point where our educational standard and quality is already at a very poor level. This is not to say that our educational standard and quality has diminished, because it has advanced tremendously, yet we still have a long ways to go if we are to join the so-called "American Political Family."

To allow this type of problem to drag on for weeks and months is a crime against our students. It is a symptom of a weak and irresponsible government. Where are our fearless leaders when we need them? What happened to all the promises of heaven that they nicely feed our citizens during time of election?

69 THE NORTHERN ISLANDS

March 31, 1977

On March 3, 1977 the NORMAR II left on a field trip to the Northern Islands and returned on Thursday, March 17th. I was fortunate to have had the opportunity to visit the Northern Islands on this trip. The ship went from Saipan to Agrigan with short stops on Anatahan, just to let some people off.

Agrigan is an island without any dock and with huge waves breaking on the shore. As a result, it was very difficult for people to land and for supplies and materials to be unloaded. The ship had to be anchored about half a mile from the shore and the people and supplies had to be taken on shore by a small boat. We spent one week on the island of Agrigan because bad weather prevented the unloading of supplies and materials.

There are approximately seven families, or forty people on Agrigan, the majority of whom are Carolinians who live in small tin houses without electricity or running water. The topography of the island is beautiful and the way of life of the people was very peaceful and relaxing. The only unpleasantness that I found was the great number of flies. Those who sit outside cannot keep their hands still because the files would be in their noses and eyes if they didn't keep moving.

While on Agrigan the NOMAR II and its officials apprehended a Japanese fishing boat which is alleged to have been travelling within the three-mile limit of the territorial waters. That ship is now anchored in Saipan and the captain is awaiting criminal prosecution in the High Court of the Trust Territory.

From Agrigan we went to Pagan where more supplies and materials were unloaded for the people there. The main thing I like about Pagan is the hot spring next to a beautiful lake in the mountains. The island has an incredibly beautiful shape. The different volcanoes and mountains and lakes are put together as in a dream. This is the only island with roads and an air strip. In has a couple of jeeps and approximately nine families. In both Agrigan and Pagan they still use the bull cart daily for their transportation.

From Pagan we proceeded to Alimagan where there are only three families living on two different parts of the island.

The ocean was so rough while we were there that most of the materials were not unloaded and the copra production was not loaded on the ship. Both Pagan and Alamagan have substantially more pigs and cattle than people. The people there definitely cannot complain of lack of food. There is more food than they can possibly consume even without any farming or domesticating of animals.

From Alamagan we went to Anatahan where there is only one family. Again the water there was so rough that it was impossible to unload supplies for the island. However, a number of people went in a small boat to an area of the island where supposedly there are lots of bats. They returned with a pretty good catch and a lot of bats were flying in the area.

The field trip is definitely not a luxurious or comfortable trip to take. The NORMAR II is the dirtiest ship I have ever seen in my life. In fact, I believe it should be junked and replaced by a more decent ship. While in Agrigan it lost one anchor and while in Alamagan one of its compressors broke down. Most of it is extremely rusty and it looks like it may fall apart any time. Even its radar equipment is broken and its radio is not reliable. In comparing NORMAR II with the Japanese ship that was apprehended it's like comparing the Office of the Resident Commissioner with the dump in Garapan.

During the trip there were no comfortable beds for people to sleep on and in most cases people went without brushing their teeth or showering for several days or weeks. The entire trip is not generally a pleasurable trip but it is a very unique, challenging, and rewarding trip. I would not encourage people to take such a trip on any ship like the NORMAR II, but I think any person who does will not regret the experience.

The particular trip which I took left much to be desired with respect to planning and operation. The trip could have taken much less time and all the supplies and cargoes could have been unloaded on the islands had there been proper planning and coordination between the ship, the stevedore, and the island people. Even the food on the ship almost ran out because there was no coordination between the number of people eating on the ship and the information provided to the cook. A lot of times the cook would cook food for fifty people when there were only twenty people on board because all the people had left for the island. Had there been good planning and good coordination, the trip would have been a lot more productive and enjoyable.

70 POTHOLES

April 14, 1977

I would like for the Marianas director of Public Works and his subordinate officials to do a favor for the public. I would like for them to take their individual cars and to drive to the Saipan International Airport using the road which leads from district #3 of Chalan Kanoa and goes by the agriculture station in As Perdido. It would be best if they follow the other car closely and travel at the regular speed with the windows of their cars open. And the same time, to also allow their children to walk from the agriculture station to the Hopwood Jr. High School while these cars are travelling on that road. The same people should then return 2 or 3 weeks after and do the same thing all over again. If these officials do what I suggest above, the public will be receiving a great favor. Let me explain why.

Supposedly this road has just been fixed by the Marianas Government. A grader has smoothed the surface of the road by scraping the dust off and depositing some of it in the holes and the rest over the entire road. With the 1 or 2 inches of dust created and deposited on the road and in the holes, the following consequences are inevitable. First, when two or more cars follow each other the cars behind will be totally covered by dust so as to suffocate and paint the driver or passengers. This makes driving very unsafe and very unhealthy. There are children who travel to the Hopwood Jr.

148

High School and the Chalan Kanoa Elementary School on foot using that road. When a car goes by the children are covered with dust and are all white by the time they get to the school. This is not only unsafe in terms of traffic, but very unhealthy and makes the children filthy by the time they get home after school. Second, by simply pushing dust into the pot holes on the road it does not fix the road for any substantial period of time. Within 2 or 3 weeks after all the dust has been blown away by the wind and the cars or washed away by the rain the big holes appear again and the 2 days at work done by the Government is worthless.

In fact, the road is not actually being fixed or repaired. Instead, the road is being ruined further and by doing so making it unsafe, unsanitary, and a waste of time and money. There is no question that this road needs to be maintained and repaired continuously. It is a very important road because most people living in Chalan Kanoa take this road to the airport and most people of Saipan live in Chalan Kanoa. In fact, this road should be given priority in any program for the paving of roads on Saipan.

The reason that I suggest the action to be taken by officials of the Public Works above, is to simply demonstrate to them the consequences of their efforts in fixing this road. The intent to fix the road is definitely good and the people are grateful for that. But the manner in which it is done is ineffective and should be changed and improved. Perhaps people living in other areas of Saipan may have the same complaints and problems. But this road is of utmost importance because of the services that it gives to the people who use the airport and to the tourists who bring substantial amount of revenue and take our image to the rest of the world. I hope that this column will be taken positively as a constructive criticism so that positive action will be taken without emotional consequences.

71 A LOVE LETTER TO THE PHONE COMPANY

January 29, 1979

I have seen the new Telephone Directory produced in very pretty colors and format. Looking at the directory itself may give one of the impression that there is progress in our telephone system. However, the fact is, our telephone system is in its worst condition and the services being given to our paying citizens is not worth the rate that is being charged.

I have a telephone that has not worked since the first week of August when we had the flood. That is in my previous residence. I have a new residence and have applied for a telephone to be installed. The application was submitted in the summer of 1977 and I was told then that the telephone would be installed by October or November of 1977. This is now 1979 , and no telephone has been installed.

There is a telephone in my office which works but which cannot be used because as soon as you pick up the telephone a very loud and irritating static noise begins. Only about twenty percent (20%) of the time, the noise would disappear and you may be able to hear the other party. If the telephone company is to be fair and equitable, perhaps it should reduce its rates by about eighty percent (80%). That will almost equal the value of the services being rendered to the customers.

Better yet, the phone system should be fixed so that we will have one that works and one worth paying for.

ABOUT THE EDITOR

Angelo O'Connor Villagomez is an avid scuba diver, lifelong Red Sox fan, and mediocre ukulele player. He's dedicated most of his life working to protect our shared ocean heritage. He lives in Washington, DC with his wife, Edz.

You can read his blog at:

www.taotaotasi.com